INTERMISSION

INTERMISSION

HOW FERVOR, FRIENDSHIPS AND FAITH TOOK ME TO THE SECOND ACT

Mindie Barnett

A POST HILL PRESS BOOK

Intermission:
How Fervor, Friendships and Faith Took Me to The Second Act
© 2020 by Mindie Barnett
All Rights Reserved
First Post Hill Press Hardcover Edition: February 2019

ISBN: 978-1-64293-428-1

Cover art by Cody Corcoran

Post Hill Press
New York • Nashville
posthillpress.com

Published in the United States of America

*I dedicate this book to the two offshoots of my soul—
my dearest Arielle Rose and my sweet Julian Rai.*

*Arielle, may this book remind you to set your sights
on the stars but be content with the gifts within reach;
and Julian, may you conquer all your challenges
and remember to always save a dance for Mommy—
no matter how big you may get.*

I love you both with every ounce of my being.

INTRODUCTION

L ast fall, my ex-husband's most recent birthday fell in the middle of the week. I invited him out to dinner the night before the actual day for a small family pre-celebration. It was my parenting time with the kids, but I wanted us all to celebrate together. I always like to have the birthday person make a wish and blow out a candle, and our waitress at the diner obliged us with a cupcake. We all sang. I snapped a cute photo of Jason with both kids and posted it on my social media, saying something like:

> *Happy early birthday, Jason, I'm really blessed that after all we've been through I can still call you family. Thanks so much for being such a great dad to these two kids.*

As the owner of a public relations firm, I post quite frequently on social media. It's the nature of my job. This particular post caused much more of a stir than usual. I got hundreds of "likes" and comments about how refreshing it was to see such a harmonious co-parenting relationship between a recently divorced couple. My friend Caryn, an elementary school teacher, commented, "I can't tell you how many parent/teacher conferences I have to conduct twice, because the parents refuse to even sit through a meeting concerning their child together. If these people would just realize how hard it is on their kids! You should teach a class!"

The light went on in my head. I had wanted to write a book for years, but just couldn't settle on the topic. "You've just inspired me to write a book!" I wrote back. "Thanks!"

I am proud of the peaceful process Jason and I managed to achieve and the way we both handled ourselves during what anyone who has ever divorced knows is probably the most trying time of your life. Co-parenting with your ex is not easy, and there's a lot of biting my tongue, sometimes until it bleeds. It's about having the strength to pick your battles. I pick and choose my arguments so it's not an ongoing war.

Now that we're divorced, there is far less obligation to concede and compromise. It's quite a bit more effort once you are no longer committed, and children are the only link left, to behave in a great way. Because you no longer have to get in bed with that person at night, share finances, see their mother the next day. You don't have to speak with them at all if you don't want to, so you really must be careful about the fighting part, or the disagreeing.

We didn't get divorced because we no longer liked each other; it just wasn't a viable long-term romantic connection. I can truthfully say today that I love Jason—probably more now than I did when we were married, in a different sort of way. We have managed to maintain great relationships with our extended families too. I still consider his parents my in-laws. Mark and Roz are wonderful grandparents to my children. I know they would do anything for me, as I would for them. My own parents do so much for me already, and I am blessed to have even more support.

At a recent dance recital for my daughter, Jason and I sat next to each other, not because we had to, but because we wanted to. We whispered to each other throughout, and I teased him a bit when I saw a woman texting him. When Jason enters into a serious relationship, I am going to do my very best to be accommodating to his girlfriend or wife. As long as she's good to my kids, I will embrace her—no matter what. I appreciate anyone who loves Jason. They should!

* * * *

Breaking up my perfect-on-paper family has been the greatest test in my life so far. I learned so much in my marriage about cohabitating and raising children with another person. I learned even more about divorcing and raising children with that same person. But my lessons were far from over after the breakup. There has been no fairy-tale ending with a new Prince Charming; I am still learning new lessons about love, and starting over, and living with myself.

I look at this time in my life as an intermission. It's a break. It isn't when the new music starts and the lights blaze on. I certainly felt lost, and some days I still do! It's not that everything in life always works out quickly and easily, and I am not saying it does. But I believe in myself and my message, and I want to inspire other women—or men!—anyone who is looking to reset and start over in a new kind of life. The things I wanted most happened for me, but truthfully, deep down I never for a moment thought they wouldn't. That attitude, more than anything else, is what I hope to pass along in this book. You will get through this, whatever it is you're facing. You absolutely can be stronger, happier, and more resilient in your second act.

Cheers!

Mindie

CHAPTER 1

A typical Monday morning in what was, in many ways, paradise. The sun was shining brightly on Mount Laurel, a picturesque town in southern New Jersey. The big house on Summit Road was in the highly desirable Ravenscliff development. A neighborhood full of impressive, family-friendly homes all set on large lots. We were surrounded by pleasant young professionals with kids, dogs, and careers in the city. There were parties and parades and Little League. We enjoyed the town park, excellent schools, safe streets, gorgeous landscapes, and high-end shopping centers. We had a twenty-minute commute to Philadelphia and it was just ninety minutes by train or car to Manhattan. Both sets of grandparents lived nearby. It was the ideal place to raise a family.

My husband, Jason, raced out the door by seven a.m., as he did every weekday. Our indispensable nanny, Alicia, was in the kitchen, feeding then-seven-year-old Arielle and three-year-old Julian breakfast. Our dog, Max, sniffed hopefully under the table, searching for dropped food. I could hear laughter and screeching and the banging of utensils from downstairs as I shut the bathroom door firmly behind me. These precious few minutes alone each morning had always been a favorite part of my day.

In a home I loved and had taken great pride in decorating, the master bathroom was my favorite room of all and a personal haven. It was painted a buttercream bisque with plush area rugs. Antique perfume bottles lined brass shelves. An over-sized Jacuzzi spotlighted by a crystal chandelier dominated the space, which was the size of a typical standard bedroom. My dream bathroom featured every possible amenity, from double sinks to a marble floor and a flat-screen TV hanging above the sunken tub. Spa products, fluffy towels, and scented candles were scattered strategically throughout. The floor-to-ceiling glass shower could easily hold four people...though it hadn't even held two for a long, long time. Water jets set at varying heights ensured a relaxing—or invigorating—spray from all directions. This shower, along with my beloved tub, was my morning indulgence.

But on this day, like so many others lately, the water beating down failed to soothe me or take the knots out of my neck and back. I knew that I couldn't go on much longer. I loved many things about my life, but my marriage was no longer one of them. I knew I needed to leave. When was I finally going to get up the nerve and tell my husband? When was I finally going to get up my courage and just go? Accustomed to acting swiftly and decisively at work, I found myself paralyzed by the enormity of this decision.

There was a mountain in front of me, one that I knew I needed to climb, but committing to that first step was just impossible. I loved my kids, and Jason and I both worked so hard to provide the very best life we could for both of them. And I knew I was blessed with an abundance of material possessions. But I could no longer convince myself this was enough. It wasn't. I was sad much of the time. I didn't feel fulfilled; I felt invisible. Bottom line? I felt alone, and as many people before me have discovered, there's nothing worse than feeling alone when you're in a partnership.

I loved my husband, but I was no longer sure I was *in love* with him. He was a caring parent, a steady and consistent presence, but the romantic, touchy-feely phase of our relationship had dissipated and died long ago. I thought of my mom and dad, still in love and showing it, well into their seventies. This was the picture I had in my mind growing up, the sort of relationship I wanted to emulate, but I didn't have that. At all. Not even close.

But was that enough of a reason to break up a family? Every morning, I thought about my beautiful home that I was justifiably proud of. My impressive bathroom. My beloved custom deck and massive backyard. My husband, who was, after all, a pretty good guy. And, as always, the deal breaker. *The kids are so comfortable and well set up here. We have a great routine; their lives are happy and stable. I can't uproot them and ruin their lives.* Defeated, I grabbed my towel, dried myself off, and put on a happy face. I dressed for the day in my most fashionable attire—a custom uniform of mine—and reentered the familiar chaos of a weekday: work, kids, clients, trips.... The daily business of life made such a major decision easy to put off. *I'll do it tomorrow*, I told myself. Like I did every day.

* * * *

I sat in my therapist's office, Kleenex in hand, going over the same old stuff. Should I stay or should I go? "You know what it's like right here, where you are," my therapist pointed out. "So, are you going to take a chance that you might be happy on the other side, or do you want to stick it out where you are? Your current situation probably won't get significantly better or worse."

The unknown is so scary; I knew very well it was what kept men and women alike in bad relationships for so long. You waited to separate until summer, which eventually turned into the new year, which then turned into once the kids get into high school. That became once they're off to college, as soon as they graduate, or once they were finally out on their own. Couples got stuck in that rut and all of a sudden, another ten years had passed, with both people still there. Stuck, uncomfortably comfortable, in the same familiar environment. Still unable to pull that trigger. I had been hovering in that place for far too long!

In the list of pros and cons that was constantly tabulated in my head, there were many compelling reasons for me to stay. Starting with the fact that my husband and I rarely even fought. Certainly, we didn't yell and scream or have big blowouts. We weren't at each other's throats all the time. But there wasn't any passion there either, no fire. I had my grievances; so did he. But was I really going to throw away what most people would call ten pretty good years, risk my kids' well-being, and take a leap of faith that maybe I'd be happier on the other side? Not yet. Not just yet. I was stuck.

In the same way that I had seen pregnant women and baby carriages everywhere when I was trying to conceive, divorce seemed to be in the air. Every morning I read all the gossip and entertainment blogs to stay up to date for my PR business. Every morning another split was breaking news. Gwen Stefani was leaving Gavin Rossdale. Jen and Ben started their long, long separation. Gwyneth Paltrow started a national conversation about "conscious uncoupling."

I could not stop reading these stories in *US Weekly* or online on the *Daily Mail's* site. Not to admire the clothes or check out the fashions, which would normally have been my focus. Not because I equated my situation in any way with what these women were facing under such a harsh spotlight. It was how they handled their divorce that got my attention...and admiration. Whatever their personal reasons, they did it. They got up the courage and did it. And got on with it!

In the spring of 2015 the tide started to shift. I saw friends making big changes in their lives. A close girlfriend got engaged; another good friend filed for divorce. Sadly, it was hearing about the divorce and not the engagement that caught my attention. Great, my friend was getting married; mazel tov. Of course, I was happy for her. But my girlfriend who was leaving her husband? I was actually jealous of her!

Late that summer Jason and I celebrated our ten-year anniversary over Labor Day weekend. I was miserable. A jeweler, Jason had offered to reset my engagement ring as my gift. I was reluctant to hand it over, because deep down inside, somewhere, I knew I might not be wearing it forever. I made weak excuses about why I couldn't take it off right now. But none of that worked and a new, dazzling setting was presented to me. He definitely was generous!

We decided to go to Washington, DC, to mark the occasion. I would have loved to be in love, slipping away with my husband on a romantic trip to celebrate ten years of coupledom. This would not be that. Because I was the planner, I brought the kids along; I knew it wasn't going to be any sort of adults-only getaway. We planned to drive from our house, a very manageable two-hour trip. I sat on a stool at the island in our enormous kitchen as the kids played in the adjoining great room and Jason brought the car around. I was texting back and forth with my girlfriend Lauren: "So upset. I am depressed. This is not where I want to be." She did her best to give me a pep talk.

The weekend was doomed. Everything went wrong from the moment we pulled out of the driveway. Both kids were cranky. Traffic was dreadful. We arrived safely and checked into the hotel, then toured a few museums. Arielle suddenly became sick and feverish, so we retreated to our room. She was so miserable that I wondered if we should just go home and seek medical attention, but then her fever broke. The second she got better, Jason succumbed to the same bug. He was deathly ill. On the date of our actual anniversary, I went out to dinner in downtown DC with my son, Julian—he was the only other healthy family member. The worst part about it was that how this all shook out was perfectly okay with me. Not a good sign!

I didn't keep these feelings bottled up inside. Jason and I talked about our marriage. All the time, he would have probably said. And he tried to listen. But at the end of the day we were just not meant to be forever. He wasn't mean. He did love me... and vice versa. But I wanted—needed—a different type of relationship. It just wasn't a great match. I think he wanted to be the person I wanted, but he could not. It wasn't in his makeup. No one can be someone they're not, at least not for long. Far better to just be yourself. After all, who else can you be?

We had "different expectations" of what a relationship should look like. We had "incompatible love and affection thresholds." Can you tell I've been through a lot of therapy?

CHAPTER 2

Back to school. Ten-year anniversary behind us, and the school year was in full swing. In New Jersey the schools close every year for a statewide teachers' convention; it usually falls a couple of weeks before Thanksgiving. Traditionally, families go away for a long weekend; with the kids off, it's the perfect opportunity for a quick trip. We took a family vacation to Disneyworld, one of our favorite destinations with the kids. We all loved Disneyworld; we had been there many times before. Never had I had such a heavy heart at the happiest place on earth. At the end of a long day, as we rode the monorail back to our hotel, I watched the fireworks explode over the castle and my eyes filled up. I knew this was the last family trip to Disneyworld. I could no longer keep up the charade.

At home I stayed busy. One day I was going about my regular business, pitching clients to various print, television, and online outlets. I reached out to the editor-in-chief of a popular regional magazine in Philadelphia. My pitch went well and my client was eventually profiled in the magazine, so I went into Philly to meet this man in person and discuss other opportunities.

Shane was fun, witty, charismatic. We hit it off immediately, in a platonic, friendly sort of way.

As things were bottoming out at home, I found myself really finding this man great to talk to—not to mention attractive. We had a number of interests in common, including time spent in the news business. I once joked with him, "You're the male me!" He quickly became a good friend and solid business contact. I truly enjoyed his company. However, I was married, and that still mattered to me. Nobody crossed any lines.

There was nothing improper about our relationship; I had many male friends. This guy, however, stirred up some feelings in me that made me very uncomfortable and hastened the end of my marriage. These were not the kind of feelings a happily married woman would be entertaining. It's not that someone came along and I was suddenly unhappy; I was unhappy and without even thinking I found myself looking at him very differently. This was a sea change, one I knew the marriage couldn't survive.

I didn't want to be feeling anything like this, but I was. It showed me, very viscerally, that there actually were other men in the world whom I might feel romantically about. They did exist and they were out there. I wanted to give myself the chance to find the kind of partnership I longed for. I also wanted my kids to see a different sort of relationship.

One night I was cleaning up after dinner, rinsing the dishes and loading the dishwasher. As I was standing at the sink, Jason came up behind me and gave me a bear hug. This was surprising; it wasn't at all his normal behavior to make such spontaneous gestures of affection. Even so, it was just a quick hug. But Arielle recoiled. "Ewwwww, Dad, gross," she said, with all the disgust a seven-year-old could muster. She wrinkled her nose and turned away. It struck me, hard. She didn't think this was normal. She was not used to that kind of display.

Later that night, I laid down with her for a few minutes at bedtime. The lights were low as we curled up under her white lace canopy. I could just make out our outlines in the mirrored doors of her huge closet. They reflected a gorgeous dollhouse. Pink satin curtains framing an expansive green lawn. Rose wallpaper, a blush rug, and oversize blocks spelling out her name. A perfect princess room, as pretty as I could make it. I rubbed her back and said casually, "Arielle, you know when Daddy hugged me tonight, that's normal. That's what parents do, right? You know that."

"Huh." She was clearly unconvinced.

"But, Arielle, you know that my mommy and daddy—your mom-mom and pop-pop—have always done that kind of thing. When you grow up, you will do that too. You will find your very own prince who will want to hug you and kiss you and be near you and love you all the time." How I prayed that would happen, that my daughter would find that kind of relationship. Unfortunately, I didn't have it myself. But I was only forty-one. My life wasn't over. It really wasn't too late for me...if I could find the courage to leave, that is.

We went away for New Year's with the kids, to a water-park-type amusement resort. The hotel was lovely. We had gotten an upgrade, which in theory would have been great. The kids had their own bunkbeds, set completely apart and behind a wall from the huge master bed. It was the perfect setup for a romantic encounter. This was no time for intimacy; I no longer even hoped for the possibility to arise. The marriage was over; I planned to tell my husband as soon as the holidays were over. "Go ahead, take the kids to the park," I told Jason. "I'll stay here and unpack all the bags, get us all set up." They happily took off, and I called my mom and lost it. "I want to leave!" I told her. I was crying hysterically, but I managed to pull it together before everyone came back. I could make it for three more nights. Our last trip together.

They all came piling back into the hotel room and tried to jump in the shower, but only ice-cold water would come out. After a visit from maintenance, we were eventually moved to another room; this one also a suite, but with a completely different layout. Two separate rooms, divided by an actual closing door. "Arielle and I are in the girls' room!" I said brightly, and I moved all our stuff to that space. This was the end. At long last, I was ready.

We came home from the trip on January 1, New Year's Day. I headed out that night for a drink with a girlfriend, Pam, who was separated at the time. She regaled me with stories of dating once again, which I didn't care about at all. "I am not worried about dating again. I just need to exit this situation, now," I told her. I needed to extricate myself from my own life.

I woke to the second day of the new year. Time to take stock. Here I was, another year, and again, nothing had changed. I was really afraid I was headed for a deep, dark depression, the kind that would hold me back from succeeding at work, from being the kind of mother I wanted to be, from taking care of my health...from truly living. I hadn't yet fallen into despair, but I was acutely aware that I needed to get proactive. Another year of inaction would absolutely push me over the edge.

That afternoon I went into New York City to catch up with another old friend who also happened to be divorced. Was this catching or what? Tracy and I had been friends for years, since working in the news business together, and she had come to town for a holiday wedding. I rarely got the chance to see her, as she now lived in Maine, so this was a treat. She had her two kids with her, and I brought Arielle. My daughter and I took the train in and made a day of lunch and shopping.

Once again, I was equivocating. Afraid to pull the trigger. As we walked along Madison Avenue, the kids skipping ahead of us, I told her, "Next week. Next week for sure."

"Mindie, just go home," Tracy said. "Go home and do it. The anticipation is so much worse than the actual act. Go home, talk to him, that's it."

I felt sick for the rest of our outing, but I also knew she was right. I was uncharacteristically quiet on our train ride home as Arielle chatted on about the day and all the fun things we had seen. Later, Jason and I put the kids to bed. Just another night at home like a thousand others. As we entered our bedroom I said, "I really need to talk to you."

He heard something in my voice. Jason came around to my side of the bed and looked at me. "I have been so unhappy, and I am still not happy." My tears started to fall. "This is so hard for me to say, but I just can't do this anymore. We need to separate."

It was horrible. To say something like that to someone you do love, who does love you, however imperfectly, is kind of like a death. This was the end, and it wasn't easy or smooth. My husband looked utterly defeated when our discussion ended. He wasn't angry, just sad. Resigned.

"I guess I'll just go sleep in the guest room," he said, and picked up his pillow. He lingered for a moment in the doorway, but all I could say was, "Okay." He padded off down the hallway. Part of me wanted to go after him, but I knew that was the wrong move. I had finally done it. I had thrown down the gauntlet. Everything was going to be different from this night forward.

Intermission had begun.

CHAPTER 3

I had been thinking about this decision for months and months, if not years. I'd considered all my options carefully; this was as far as it could be from a spur-of-the-moment thing. Still, once I made my big announcement, I wasn't at all sure what was going to happen next. Was Jason going to move out or what? I took things very cautiously. I was all right with taking baby steps. In fact, I thought it was the best way for us to proceed.

There was no coming back from this decision, that much I knew, so I felt it was best for all of us, especially the kids, to understand what life would be like each step of the way. We started with a "time out" and having daddy move permanently to the guest room. That was hard. Then we had to face the realities of what divorce would bring: dividing properties and making new living arrangements. That was harder.

Naturally, once the shock and sorrow wore off, anger showed through. Jason proved surprisingly stubborn about actually physically separating. He absolutely put his foot down and refused to leave. I wasn't about to leave either, so it was a stalemate. We both remained under one roof. On weekends, one of us acted as the parent at home in charge. If it was my weekend, he headed to his parents' place. On his weekends, I went to our condo at the shore or my own parents' home.

This living arrangement went on from January for several months, and annoying as it was to have us both in the family house, it spurred me on to make the next move. Divorce. This came as a blow to Jason, as he was trying for a reconciliation, doing his best to pull things back together. He was really making an effort, and many days I was sorely tempted to forget this whole separation thing.

A big part of me wanted to try again, if only for the kids' sake. But we had tried that. We'd been trying that for a few years now. It wasn't working; it wasn't going to work. It was time to go, as simple as that. Our act was over. It had taken so much to get to this point of "separation." I didn't trust that I could do it again if we reconciled.

Eventually Jason came to me. "Either you commit to working on our marriage or we divorce."

"I think we should get divorced," I told him. I had already seen an attorney, just to educate myself on the process and line up somebody to work with, but we agreed to mediate instead of litigate. We booked a couple of private sessions, and in the end, we didn't really have much to fight about. He wanted the kids for as much time as he could possibly have them, and so did I. It was wrenching to let them go at all, of course, but if we could come to an arrangement all the rest was basically a done deal. We wouldn't have to endure a long, messy, expensive court battle.

The custody issue was a bit sticky; I was hoping for more time than I settled for, but I knew in my heart Jason was a loving father who deserved equal time with his kids. I never wanted them to resent me for "taking" their dad away. I sucked it up, for everyone's sake, though it was excoriatingly painful. Not having my small kids around for half the time was a true knife in my heart. Almost to the point I thought I might waver. Still, I held on.

I had told Jason I wanted to get divorced in April, and the deed was done by the end of June. It was the fastest divorce imaginable; my lawyer remarked that he had never seen any case move through the system so quickly. June 23 was a beautiful summer day. I drove to the courthouse in Mount Holly, New Jersey, as we were residents of Burlington County. I was dressed in a very conservative, navy pinstripe suit dress. I got a text from Jason as I pulled into the lot. "I'm gonna throw up," it said.

Jason met me on the steps and we walked into the courthouse together. My lawyer was present, mainly because someone had to file the papers. He saw us enter, came up to me, and pulled me away. "Come with me, Mindie," he said. "There are a couple of last-minute things we need to go over." The two of us retired to a small private room.

"I didn't really need to go over anything. This is going to be hard enough; don't sit and chat with him. You might change your mind," he said, only half-jokingly. He was right. I was very emotional. Teary, questioning myself, wondering what I'd done.

The judge called us in. Jason and I stood together in front of the judge, just as we'd stood in front of the rabbi when we married. The hearing was brief and businesslike. When our marriage was disposed of, I had to stay for another separate hearing because I wanted to drop my married last name and return to my maiden name, Barnett. Another stop in front of the judge, some more paperwork, and my birth name was restored. I was divorced. It was done.

As I got into my car outside the courthouse my phone beeped. Jason again. "This is the worst day of my life. I feel like someone died." I closed my eyes and held back the tears. It was a very sad day. I was not feeling at all happy or liberated or "go, girl!"

That night I poured out my heart on social media. The words tumbled out of me in a long post I called "The First Day." I wrote all about how one door had closed, another was opening; how grateful I was for all the memories in my marriage, good and bad. They had made me the person I was. Now I was tentatively excited for the person I would become.

* * * *

Acting on the advice of the attorney, we did not put our house on the market until we had hashed out our settlement with the mediator, in writing. This was to avoid any fighting at a time when feelings would be running high. By the time we had our settlement agreement completed, it was mid-May, which meant the ideal home-selling time in the suburbs had passed. People in our community—which was very much a family neighborhood, mostly couples with children—who wanted to make a move that year had already done so. The time to put your house on the market, our real estate agent informed us, was right after Christmas. That way, by summertime everyone was in the new house, adjusting to the new neighborhood and ready for school at summer's end. Well, too late for that. We missed the boat.

We got an offer from a woman who was going through her own divorce, but her financial arrangements fell through, so that offer vanished. The breakup was lurching along. Though we'd been officially divorced in June, we didn't sell the house until October. I was willing to abide by the schedule we had hammered out, but my now ex-husband suddenly didn't want to leave on "my" days. I wasn't about to be the only one the kids saw leaving all the time, so we both stayed. The process was excruciating, and I was no longer regretting my decision. I was starting to hate him, and no doubt vice versa. Imagine living full time with your ex in separate rooms, taking on tasks like dividing furniture and wedding gifts on weekends. It was a very difficult time.

Tensions were exacerbated by our final family vacation. In an optimistic moment I had booked a trip to Puerto Rico earlier that year, paid for it in full and nonrefundable, before finally asking for the divorce. By the time we left on a weeklong trip, I was dreading it. I didn't want to go, but I didn't want to not go either. I was thinking maybe we should try to divide the trip and have one of us there for the first half, with the second parent showing up to take over the rest of the time. That would have been too complicated, and life was complicated enough, so we eventually got two rooms with an adjoining door.

Finally, an offer came through on the house, and fittingly enough, we closed on Halloween. The day we closed was a shock. Even though we were officially, on paper, divorced, we had yet to truly separate. We still had dinners together during the week and showed up for activities together, both of us doing our absolute best to minimize the effects on the kids. The day we officially closed on the house was so sad. As Jason drove me to the title office to sign the final papers, I was crying. "You wanted this," he said grimly.

"I wasn't happy! It wasn't working! I didn't *want this*, as you put it. There was only one person fighting for this marriage, and that was me. Come on. I never *wanted* to get divorced." I shook my head and slumped in the seat.

We all moved out on the first of November, 2016. Jason and I headed to different homes in the nearby town of Voorhees. And though I loved my new house, it was certainly a huge, abrupt change. That first night, as I walked around, I became overwhelmed with panic. I was now the sole owner of a good-size single-family home. Meaning in charge of the yard, the filters, the heater, the electricity.... Whatever went wrong, it was up to me to fix it or get it fixed. I should have rented, like my mom suggested, so all that stuff would be someone else's problem. Or just bought a condo. This was way too much. My mind raced; I couldn't relax. My first night on my brand-new mattress was sleepless.

My faith was restored in the morning. I woke up and the world looked brighter. We had a new home, in a great school district, and my ex and I were both committed to our kids' well-being. Jason was five minutes away to ensure as little disruption to their lives as possible. Everything was going to be all right. That weekend the kids and I held our first family Shabbat on Friday evening, just the three of us. I was anxious to establish some new family traditions. It was wonderful. It was peaceful. The next weekend was a little tougher; I didn't have the kids. As I walked in the door the house was so quiet. It felt strange to be all alone there.

For the first time in years I was...all...by...myself. I was free to do whatever I wanted. I could go to the gym. See a friend. Watch TV. Anything. Having been on the mommy track for the past eight years, I was accustomed to very little time to myself. The sudden freedom was overwhelming. I walked through my new house, still with boxes in some corners. This was my space, to do with whatever I pleased. Where I would invite over whomever I pleased. I met my parents for dinner that night and we toasted to new beginnings. It was time to begin my second act.

That was it.... The speediest divorce ever, as my lawyer noted. But there was so much more that led up to it, got me through it, steadied me in the times ahead. Behind the scenes was the rest of the story.

Power Passage #1

READ!

"Today a reader, tomorrow a leader."

—MARGARET FULLER

I perused divorce memoirs and relationship guides during my separation. Not too many, mainly because I felt like a lot of those books were directed at women who were really down and embittered and in a terrible place. That's not me, and it never was me. I wasn't lost; I was never completely devastated. I didn't come out of my divorce disenchanted with men or with life overall. I am grateful for every gift, mainly my two amazing kids, which are the product of my marriage. I learned a great deal. In short, I look for the lessons and appreciate them all, because they've made me who I am today.

Here, in no particular order, are some books that have helped me reflect, search my soul, or handle life a bit differently, in a new and better way:

Einstein and the Rabbi: Searching for the Soul, by Naomi Levy, is all about the soul: that "very deep place inside us. A place of emotional truth." In this accessible and well-written book by a female rabbi, she discusses how, in these uncertain times, to find, nurture, and nourish our souls. Part memoir, part spiritual guide, and part gripping historical mystery, this is like no other self-help book you will ever read! Packed full of valuable Jewish lore and wisdom, the rabbi shares stories from her own life and those of her congregation to illuminate love, marriage, grief, overcoming setbacks, parenting, and so much more. It will resonate with those of all faiths…or just those seeking warm and wise guidance on living happily and authentically.

The Miracle Morning: The Not-So-Obvious Secret Guaranteed to Transform Your Life (Before 8AM), by Hal Elrod. Author/motivational coach Elrod has overcome some major obstacles. He survived a horrendous car accident when he was twenty, and defied doctors who said he would never walk again. He wrote his first book, but his publisher bankrupted him and left the country, leaving him broke and depressed. Then his fiancée left him. He couldn't even get out of bed after that one. Someone told him to go running, and he did, eventually running a marathon. (Like me!) He has taken all these life lessons and more to create an innovative program for success. In a nutshell, it's about getting excited about your own life and waking up each day with anticipation. I do my best to regularly follow his morning ritual; it incorporates affirmations, visualization, exercise, and reading. This program is so worth the hour every morning! (There's a twenty-minute version for when you're traveling, pressed for time, or just a sleep-deprived mom.)

Dear Martha: WTF?: What I Found in My Search for Why, by Tricia LaVoice, is a compelling memoir by a truly original new voice. LaVoice navigates terrible grief, marriage, friendship, parenting, loss, and love with the help of a beautiful tree named

Martha in her Connecticut backyard. Yes, really…. Go with the unusual premise and you will be rewarded by insights that will be appreciated by all women.

Night, by Elie Wiesel. It's important to study the Holocaust for many reasons, mostly to remind us all: never again. In this classic work, Wiesel relates the incredible story of his improbable survival after being deported to Auschwitz from his native Romania. Though most of his family died in the camps, he was eventually freed from Buchenwald at age seventeen. Night is a short, deceptively simple but incredibly powerful meditation on man's inhumanity to his fellow man. Wiesel won the Nobel Peace Prize for his life's work of bearing witness to these horrors; it is our duty to read his testimony. When you feel life is unbearable, read this; it will quickly put things in their proper perspective.

Leaders Eat Last, by Simon Sinek. I didn't study business in school, and never thought I would own my own company, so I'm always looking to learn from others. Speaker and writer Sinek describes himself as an optimist who teaches people to inspire others. After I read his books and watched his TED talks, I am a believer. His advice is commonsense but valuable for anyone looking to become a leader. As someone always looking to polish my business skills and leadership ability, I felt motivated and ready to charge after finishing this book.

CHAPTER 4

started dancing at a very early age. I was in ballet lessons at age two, on pointe at fourteen. It seemed like a natural fit to try out for cheerleading when I entered Shawnee High School in my hometown of Medford, New Jersey. The innate ability was there, and I was certainly perky enough. The problem was that many of the other girls in my freshman class had been cheering for a long time, throughout middle school and, even, in some cases, all the way back to elementary school. When I tried out but failed to make the football cheerleading squad, I was devastated. This was a serious blow in my adolescent life. I had really wanted it, had worked hard for it, and, to add insult to injury, several of my friends made the twelve-member squad.

I came home from school depressed the day the results were posted. My parents, who had just walked in themselves from work, met me at the door, ready to console. They had watched me practicing for tryouts with my friends, who were all very experienced. Those girls knew how to cheer and hold certain positions and tumble and build pyramids and fly through the air. It had been pretty obvious, looking back, that my parents had seen this disappointment coming. That night at the dinner table I sat moping like only a fourteen-year-old girl can. Pushing my food around on the plate, too upset to eat. My dad, a veteran high school principal who had seen it all, made a suggestion.

"Mindie, on Monday, stay after school and ask the coach if you can just talk with her for a few minutes. Tell her you want to know what to work on, so you'll be better prepared for winter tryouts, for the basketball cheerleading team."

That was an alien, intimidating idea. Miss Oberg was not a warm and fuzzy nurturer. She was the very image of a tough, no-nonsense phys ed teacher. She could shut down a group of rowdy high school boys...or girls...in a second. I was sure she would be less than delighted to chat with me, but after a weekend of despair, talking on the phone to my friends who had made the squad, and tossing and turning, I decided, why not. I was afraid, very afraid, but I decided to do it anyway.

That Monday after school I stood outside the coach's closed office door. My hands were shaking; I was sweating. I really did not want to do this. But I screwed up all my courage and knocked. She jerked the door open and as soon as she saw me, an annoyed look flitted across her face. The coach had no doubt spent the day on the phone with a number of irate parents asking why their perfect daughter hadn't made the squad. It was that kind of school, with plenty of that kind of parent. But I wasn't thinking of that at the time; her forbidding look just made me want to run away. "Please, Miss Oberg, can I speak to you for a minute about how I can improve, so I can hopefully do better next tryout and make the squad next time?" I squeaked out.

"Mindie, it was extremely competitive this year," she said. I knew that; I'd been there, along with the other seventy-four girls at tryouts.

"Yes, and I know it will be competitive next time too. I'm hoping to pick up some tips on what to focus on. How to make a better showing next time."

Her face softened just a bit. "Come with me," she said. "I'm headed to practice. During breaks, we can talk for a bit." I followed her out into the perfect fall day, where the newly chosen squad was doing drills down on the field. How badly I wished I was one of them! But I sat in the first row of the stands, sucked it up, and watched and waited. During breaks, I listened to every word she said.

The coach warmed up considerably once she realized I wasn't there to complain that it wasn't fair or whine about why I hadn't been picked. Medford was an affluent area, where many kids were given a car for their seventeenth birthday. While I too was very lucky to have many comforts, I was aware how blessed I was. I didn't have an attitude; I always wanted to be friends with everybody. Being a mean girl was just not in my makeup—nor was that feeling of entitlement—and I think Miss Oberg saw that. She liked the fact that I was taking notes, writing everything she said down in a spiral notebook.

I sat quietly, observing the entire two hours. After she called an end to practice, the girls ran off to the locker room. I stood up, closed my notebook, and said, "Thank you so much for your time. I appreciate all the advice. I will see you at the next tryouts."

"Mindie," she called as I started to walk away. I turned back. "Would you like to be our team mascot? We used to have one, a long time ago, and I was thinking of bringing the tradition back. As the mascot you could practice with the team, learn all the cheers, and be in a much better place for basketball cheerleading tryouts."

"Yes! I'll do it!" I said. I was thrilled. I was now the official Shawnee Renegades mascot! "Mascot" wasn't nearly as bad as it could have been; I didn't have to dress up as a "furry" with an animal head. In fact, I got to wear a cute little cheer skirt topped with a sweatshirt my mom made for me, with fringe all over it...to suggest a Native American theme. I looked enough like a cheerleader to make me happy. Best of all, I got to cheer alongside the other girls, and they put me in all the stunts!

The only downside to this were the comments from the mean girls in my class. There were more than a few snide remarks and eyerolls the first Friday before game day when I showed up at school in my outfit. Cheerleaders were cool; a mascot was most definitely not. But I had an end goal in mind. I wanted to be a cheerleader; no, I was *going* to be a cheerleader. I could not have cared less what a few bitchy ninth graders had to say to me or about me. And after a week the snarky remarks were hushed completely anyway.

I fully embraced being a mascot. I wore my uniform with pride. I also worked my butt off at practices, twice as hard as the other girls, because I needed to. I had some catching up to do. At basketball cheer tryouts at the end of fall, as I finished my routine with a flourish, I was satisfied. I had done everything I could to improve myself; I had rehearsed endlessly, and I had done the absolute best I could. I left it all out there on the floor...and I made the squad! I was very aware that many of my teammates were technically more talented. But a couple of the girls from football cheerleading got dropped from the squad... for attitude. For being too cool for practice. For thinking they were above working for it, really. That would never be me!

By the end of the year, in fact, I was team captain. For the next four years, I cheered every season and even made my college team. That was my first experience of working for something, doing all I thought I could, not getting it, then turning around and working even harder. It was an excellent life lesson for a teenager about succeeding and reaching goals.

There had been seventy-five girls at those first football cheerleading tryouts that day in ninth grade. Only four months later, at winter basketball cheerleading tryouts, there were less than forty, about half the original number. That's because the girls who didn't make the squad on their first attempt slunk away, never to be seen again. They gave up. It was going to take so much more to make me give up on my dreams!

CHAPTER 5

Ever since I was a little girl, I have loved performing. I have loved being onstage. I have loved being in the spotlight. Singing, dancing, acting...I love all of it! Like many kids with that bent, when people asked what I wanted to do when I grew up, I would say, "I'm going to be an actress." No one was surprised. As I grew older, I found that I also loved to write. From my very first writing assignments in grade school, I wanted more. I excelled in English classes.

Our high school radio show was called "Shawnee Digest," and I served as a reporter, working alongside the main anchor and chemistry teacher Mr. Steinmetz. I interviewed the principal and other school officials for whatever might be the news of the day at school. I absolutely loved it. Shawnee High School was very cliquey, with athletics being the top of the heap as the cool thing to do. I was a cheerleader but by no means any kind of athletic star. Reporting on-air for "Shawnee Digest" was a pretty geeky activity, one all my "cool" friends looked askance at...but I didn't care. I enjoyed it. I did it anyway. It was my first taste of journalism: reporting a story, writing up the news, and then delivering it on the morning a.m. newscast—and I got hooked!

Q102 Philadelphia played the biggest hits of the nineties and had an incredible morning show. Back in the day it was *the* hot station. On assignment for my mass-media class, I went into the city to interview the hosts: Chris Jagger of "Jagger in the Morning," and his sidekick, Dirty Diana. Chris was super tall, very cool, with long hair. I observed as he and Diana broadcast their show and bantered back and forth. I was then given a tour of the station and loaded down with all the merchandise—T-shirts, tickets, and cassette tapes—I could carry. It was fantastic! Chris and Diana graciously sat for an interview as I pulled out my handheld recorder with its mini cassette tape and my reporter's notebook. It was all very official.

My piece was about the business of radio; specifically, how stations are formatted. Why certain stations would switch overnight from, say, oldies to country. Hip-hop to top forty. Classical to all-talk. I learned that in radio, deejays go where the job opening is, not necessarily to the kind of music they prefer. They had to become accustomed to showing up at their longtime job one day, learning it was switching formats the next, and being put out on the street with no notice. Even a contract wouldn't necessarily protect them when station ownership changed hands.

Sure enough, Chris would soon leave Q102 to head to a rock station in Dallas for the remainder of his career. In any case, it sounded like a tenuous profession to me. I realized that a radio career was too precarious, and though I could see what fun they had, there was not enough of a serious news focus for me.

* * * *

The Miss Burlington County (NJ) Pageant is the preliminary beauty pageant for the title of Miss New Jersey; Miss New Jersey goes on to represent the state at the Miss America Pageant. The beauty pageant world, and Miss America in particular, has come under a firestorm of criticism in recent years. The entire board of directors has been replaced, and the swimsuit competition has been eliminated. Some changing and updating to the institution was absolutely necessary, but I have nothing but good things to say about my time competing. I found the experience to be tremendous and it provided me with a solid foundation for my professional future.

My mother entered me into the Miss Burlington County Pageant while I was still in high school. Lo and behold, when I arrived at the first meeting, there was my best friend, Heather, whose mother had had the same idea. We were contestants together. Miss Burlington County was set up to run exactly on the Miss America model, with the same categories and scoring systems. I loved the "artistic expression" category: an opportunity to perform and sing onstage! The "presentation and community achievement" category, in which each girl stood behind a podium to be grilled by a panel of judges shooting rapid-fire questions, was not nearly as enjoyable.

As an aspiring journalist, I was held to a high standard. The judges questioned me about local politics, community issues, statewide concerns, and national current events. I studied every newspaper under the sun and did my best to sound informed and intelligent, but I was utterly terrified! I had far more than enough on my plate just trying to promote my platform, smile seamlessly, and look good. This interview was like the toughest job interview imaginable, not fun for a high school kid but invaluable training for what lay ahead. The judges weren't mean, but this was not any softball interview. Pageant winners must remain poised under pressure! In my first competition I did not place at all. I was, however, given a good deal of constructive criticism by the judges, who encouraged me to try again. I received some helpful advice, including a recommendation to go along more traditional lines for my song selection. I took it to heart. This sort of training was in addition to all the valuable beauty tips I picked up, everything from how to use masking tape for instant cleavage to using butt glue to keep a swimsuit firmly in place. Yes, butt glue is a real product; it comes in a can like hairspray and really works. Getting a wedgie while walking the stage in your swimsuit and clear plastic stiletto shoes is a big fashion nightmare!

There are literally dozens of different preliminary pageants going on in every town and county in the country—which are associated with the Miss America Organization and are preliminary competitions for the state title. It's an entire industry and some women make it a lifestyle. I stuck to Miss Burlington County each spring...and entered a total of three times. I never really had any expectations that I would compete at the national level, though that would have been amazing, but I had hopes for a possible Miss Burlington County title and a run in the Miss New Jersey Pageant. That would have meant significant exposure, and even more scholarship money than I was competing for at the hyperlocal level, but honestly, I did it for fun.

The next year I came in fourth place; on my third go-around I came in third. I could not have gathered the poise and confidence I had later in life without this invaluable experience. I highly recommend pageants for young women, especially given that the industry continues to evolve. What's in your head and heart are much more highly prized than what is visible in the mirror. Pageant experience gave me an edge!

* * * *

I knew I was meant for a career in broadcasting. I only applied to schools with strong communications or journalism departments, and settled on Hofstra University, where I was accepted into their School of Communication and became very involved with their broadcast journalism program. Hofstra had its own television station, HTV. As a freshman reporter, my first assignment was covering the men's soccer team. Not that I knew a thing about soccer. I didn't let that slow me down.

Attending Hofstra widened my horizons. I joined a Jewish sorority, suddenly had many more Jewish friends, and became much more influenced by Judaism than I had ever been.

I spent my entire childhood in a very WASPy town. Medford was a lovely place to grow up, but it was not particularly conducive to Jewish influence in my life. My family—Mom, Sandy, Dad, Rick, younger sister Carolyn, and I—lived a pretty secular existence. My parents belonged to a temple in another town; we used to carpool with the other two Jewish families in the area. There were more than two families, of course, but we were definitely the minority. We attended synagogue sporadically, showing up mainly for only the major holidays: Rosh Hashanah, Yom Kippur...the big ones, with days off from school.

I vividly recall that as most of my second-grade classmates were preparing for their confirmations, I was the only one attending Hebrew school, in preparation for my bat mitzvah. I hated every minute of it; the boring lessons, the time I had to spend in another classroom. I complained endlessly to my parents; eventually they relented. I quit, happily, and never looked back. There wasn't much reason to.

Some Hofstra students spent their junior year abroad. One of my sorority sisters, Megan, was headed for London; another friend, Tara, suggested Israel. Such a visit had never occurred to me. Still, this time the word *Israel* stirred something inside. Imagining going to Israel evoked feelings of longing and curiosity.

When I discussed it with my parents, they pointed out the obvious advantages of London. The language would be the same—that was the big one. Not to mention it was closer, cheaper, and easier in every way. Still, as my father said, "You may never get this opportunity again; as an aspiring news professional, you should absolutely go. Career goals aside, just being Jewish, it's important you go."

I was accepted into the program at Tel Aviv University, along with Tara. As our departure date loomed, she suddenly withdrew from the trip. There were other students going, many of them, but none from my school, so I felt like now I'd really be on my own. For a moment I reconsidered London; I could still get in. But then I decided to embrace the challenge. It was time to learn to stand on my own. Lean on myself. Stretch and grow.

Then we learned that the trip was overbooked and I wasn't going to get housing on campus. A bunch of us were left scrambling for accommodations. I was told the organizers would try to put me up in a hotel along with other students left, essentially, homeless. My mother jumped into action immediately. Through her contacts at a temple, where she taught preschool, she tracked down a man from our area who happened to live near Tel Aviv.

As luck would have it, he even had rooms available to rent in his apartment. However, he lived in Herzliya, a suburb located right on the beach. This would mean being far away from campus, requiring a daily commute on public transportation. Still, we made arrangements for my stay. Once I heard the words *on the beach* nothing would have kept me from going! Via a friend at Hofstra, I also connected with another woman who was left without dorm accommodations, Lori. She took the other vacant room in the apartment and together we braved living alone in a strange city and faraway land. She and I became fast friends, and we remain close to this day.

CHAPTER 6

Israel was a culture shock in every way. For the first three months of my stay, January to March, the air was chilly and damp because it rained all the time. Constantly. Israelis were far ahead of the "green" curve, having installed solar power panels on the roofs of most apartments, homes, and public buildings. Unfortunately, that didn't work so well during the long rainy season. Solar power meant a freezing cold shower every morning, for starters.

The apartment on the beach was not quite what I had envisioned after years of watching American TV shows like *Baywatch* and *Beverly Hills, 90210.* It was a glorified hostel, basically, though certainly in a beautiful area. But after I saw the campus dorms, I was grateful that I had lost the housing lottery. Standards were different; there was much less attention paid to comfort, let's put it that way. But I needed to be shaken up, taken out of my comfort zone. I was a coddled American college student, and I knew it.

The Israelis were wonderfully warm underneath a some-times gruff exterior. And they were such beautiful people, with perfect olive complexions, everyone in the most amazing shape from the healthful diet and lots of exercise. Lori and I took classes Sunday through Thursday, catching a local bus to campus each morning. We used to covertly study the Israeli passengers on our ride into Tel Aviv.

Those Israeli girls, with their shiny, black gorgeous hair, really knew how to dress. Even in their army uniforms, they looked amazing. I would typically rock my full nineties wear, usually shiny tracksuits that were the height of fashion back then on Long Island. Bright gold XO necklaces and toggle bracelets. Huge hoop earrings; some kind of trendy designer sneakers.

These girls were our same age, but infinitely more sophisti-cated. They were just so stylish. The way they held their bags. Their uniforms always immaculately pressed. Even in combat boots, they looked like they were on a fashion shoot, very trendy. Unlike the American military, where everybody looked exactly the same and blended into one huge indistinguishable group, these girls had elaborate hairstyles and scrunchies on their wrists to boot. They were all unique, all stunning and the men were even better.

Lori and I needed to be able to communicate right away. Whatever we wanted—to shop in the grocery store, try to read a newspaper, ride the bus—we needed to be able to say so. No one in our neighborhood spoke English, and we needed to shop and eat and get to the university, for starters. Though I had taken two semesters of Hebrew in college, I hadn't grasped enough to speak fluently. I frantically tried to recall my lessons. I could identify some of the letters on signs, and I remembered a bit about sentence construction. Slowly, painfully, we made our way. It was full and immediate immersion, for sure, and it worked. By the time the semester was over, I could speak conversational Hebrew and translate most of what I heard.

* * * *

Back home, whenever I went to an ATM on the street to take out cash, I was a little nervous. I always kept my guard up, even though I was generally in safe, suburban neighborhoods. I was accustomed to the courtesy of giving others space; that is, standing at least six feet back from the person in front of me as they made a withdrawal and looking away during their transaction to give them privacy. At home, no one wanted to hover. In Israel, the other customers crowded right up against me, waiting impatiently for me to finish. They didn't feel the need for that buffer zone of personal space, because they didn't feel unsafe. Israelis did not steal from each other...ever.

At the end of a workday or in the afternoons, when some shops closed for a break, the owners would simply slide shut a gate and lock it behind them when they had to leave. It would have been easy for passersby to stick a hand inside and grab fruit, for example, or a candy bar or a magazine; goods were easily within reach. But it didn't happen. No one would steal from a local shopkeeper, not even kids as a prank. Surrounded by mortal enemies, Israelis supported each other. Their genuine love and respect for each other, at least in that way, amazed me.

As an aspiring journalist, I was all too aware that Americans seemed to kill each other over nothing every single day without a second thought. To watch an American newscast made crime seem epidemic. I have never felt safer than I did in Israel. Not once did I ever hear about a grisly murder or robbery on the news like I did nightly at home. Walking around by myself, a young American woman, I felt fine. Of course, the terrorist aspect and heightened tension of simply living in Israel were scary enough. But day-to-day worries about personal safety were nonexistent.

* * * *

In March, the rainy season stopped and the famous sun came out. The weather was absolutely gorgeous; very hot, but dry, like in Arizona. I studied my lessons by the pool on campus or under the many palm trees. The food was delicious and super healthy: lots of fish and salads…the original Mediterranean diet, for sure. I was tan and glowing and happy.

This country was just so beautiful. As students, we took plenty of trips. We loved Netanya, a beach town in northern Israel. In Haifa, on the border of Beirut, we saw all the historic sights. We climbed Masada, and we bathed in the Dead Sea. In the southernmost part of Israel was Eilat; across the Red Sea was Jordan on the horizon. This is the resort area, full of Europeans, absolutely gorgeous. Very elegant and touristy, restaurants, stores, a booming nightlife. Dahab was a beach town in Egypt near Eilat. I left the country then, and again for a weekend in Cairo, where I saw the pyramids, King Tut's tomb, and the sphinx. I was in living history; it was amazing, but still, we were kids having fun.

Ronnie was an Israeli guy from Queens attending Tel Aviv University with me. One night, as we were out in a nightclub in Tel Aviv, he introduced me to his cousin Ayal. I was wearing my gold satin miniskirt with a form-fitting white tee. I liked to dress up, so Israel was perfect for me. Every day was a fashion show there, and Ayal fit right in. Skin-tight jeans, tan, muscles bulging out of his T-shirt, cigarette dangling out of his mouth... my very own hot Israeli!

Ayal was a bit older than we were; he had already finished his compulsory military stint. He had cut everyone's hair in the Israeli Army and was now a successful "beauty," as he introduced himself in his mangled English. He meant beautician. He was a high-end hairstylist with his own salon.

Ayal had a car, which was a big deal in Israel; most people drove around on scooters, similar to mopeds. Ayal managed to obtain what looked like an IROC Camaro, a classic muscle car, and he would speed around while blasting his music at top volume. When we started dating, he used to pick me up after class in his car. My friends were openmouthed, watching me disappear in a cloud of smoke and the roar of the engine.

We had quite a whirlwind romance for six weeks; that is, until I needed to refresh my highlights. I was obsessed with my hair, always...and the roots were growing in. How lucky, I had my very own boyfriend to do my highlights! He took me to his salon, and I cautioned him, "Not too blond, now. Just more golden highlights for contrast. I just want to get rid of these roots."

"Mindie, my sweetie," he shushed me, "I know what I am doing. All will be well." I sat back and let him do his thing, reading European fashion magazines. An hour later, he took out the foils, washed my hair, and blew it dry. I looked into the mirror and saw Chrissy Snow from *Three's Company*. My hair wasn't golden blond; it was platinum. I could not believe it.

"What have you done?" I cried. My hands flew to my head in the mirror's reflection.

"I like blonds," he said implacably. I was steaming. That was the downside of Ayal, that I'd noticed before: he wanted what he wanted...period. Forget what I wanted. That was the end of Ayal. He had been a little too fast for me anyway. He had a certain idea of fast, free, American girls in his mind. There may have been some around, but I was assuredly not one of them. We parted ways, but my blond hair remained as a souvenir. Of course, the roots that grew in were horrendous, and I had no choice but to keep them touched up. I didn't want to try to fix the mess until I got home. My parents did a double take when I got off the plane!

* * * *

Israel is a home to every religion: Islam, Christianity, Judaism. We went to Har Habayit, or Temple Mount, a sacred Jewish site. To see and hear the faithful praying at the wall—actually chanting their prayers—was so incredibly beautiful; it moved me in the way hearing the national anthem does. It stirs the soul...anybody's soul!

My friends Lori and Amy and I stood there in light summer dresses (pants are forbidden at the Wall) praying on Shabbat. It was a perfect May evening, warm and mild. The sun was setting into a magnificent purple with streaks of sun. All the Hasidic people were praying—davening—with their holy books. The sight was unforgettable; I felt an immense sense of peace and love and belonging. Our outing was followed by a communal Shabbat dinner at a rabbi's home in Jerusalem.

Israel was a profoundly life-changing trip. I don't think a day goes by that I don't think about the influence it has had on me, and how it changed me into the person I have become.

Power Passage # 2

LAUGH, DANCE, SING

"On with the dance! Let joy be unconfined."
—LORD BYRON

One of the therapists I saw as I agonized about leaving my marriage focused on building up my self-esteem and encouraging me to seek some joy in my everyday life. She made the obvious but helpful suggestion that I carve out time for activities whose only purpose was to make me happy. Performing was what had made me happiest my whole life. It was time to return to song and dance.

I have been a ballet dancer since starting lessons at the age of two at Fay Schanne's Dance Studio. That was the earliest age they took students. I studied ballet until I went on pointe, adding jazz and modern in middle school. I continued ballet dancing throughout my life, until Arielle was born. Then I took a break for a couple of years. The one thing I had never gotten around to was learning to tap dance. I enrolled in an evening adult tap class at the dancing school I was now sending my daughter to. The therapist had been right; it was a fun break for me every week. I felt happy and free again, at least for an hour and a half.

It was quite a surprise for all my mommy friends who showed up on recital night to see their children. There I was, tapping away…not at all what they were expecting. "Mindie, you're so good!" they all exclaimed afterward. I appreciated the affirmation. Then I moved on to hip-hop, something really different and unusual. It took me out of myself, which was exactly what I was seeking.

Singing, of course, goes hand in hand with dance; I did a great deal of it growing up. It was all a piece of performing, where I was somewhat of a triple threat: singing, dancing, and acting. I was the lead in the fifth-grade musical *Pinocchio* and never slowed down. Drama all through middle school, which included singing, along with outside vocal training. *Bye Bye Birdie, Annie, The Sound of Music*…. At my beloved Camp Louise overnight camp, I was in all the musical shows. I played Maria in *West Side Story*, and my father was really impressed. "You have to do something with this ability," he said, which was the genesis for my interest in broadcasting, a profession that fused all my interests.

All through high school I did shows as well. My senior year we performed *Grease*. Heather, my best friend and fellow cheerleader, was Sandy. I was Patty Simcox, the obnoxious cheerleader girl with the most school spirit at Rydell High. It was a small but showy part, and I made the most of it. I really got into character and won a local theater competition for high school actors. Performing sure made me happy!

I always sang the national anthem in every small city where I anchored the news, for the local teams of the city. In Wilmington,

Delaware, I was invited to perform at their minor league base-
ball games frequently.

I sang at my own wedding; I showed up for a practice session
the week before with the band. The bandleader offered me a
job on the spot. It was so fun that I agreed; when I returned from
my honeymoon he sent me a stack of CDs of love songs and top
forty hits. Jason saw me practicing, and said, "Mindie, you do
realize weddings are all held on weekends, right? This will mean
being away every weekend night."

"It won't be every weekend, just when they need me."

"They're going to take all your weekends. Don't you want
to spend time with me?" I did. I wanted to build our new life
together, so I regretfully declined the offer. Being a wedding
singer was not meant to be.

At Julian's Little League opener, a local woman sang the
anthem to start the season. The light went on in my head; my
daughter knew what I was thinking. "Oh no, Mom," Arielle
said worriedly. "You're not doing that!" I sure wanted to! So,
I contacted a friend, a prominent entertainment publicist who
does a lot of work with the city of Philadelphia. "I want to put
my hat in the ring to sing the national anthem at a Phillies game
this summer."

He was surprised. "Mindie, I never knew you had pipes!"

"Yes, I do. Well, at least I think I do," I said.

"Well, send me a video, let me see!" Arielle recorded me on
my phone and I sent it along, feeling a little embarrassed, but I
was thrilled when he called to say, "Hey, you're really good!" On
the basis of that short homemade video alone, I was invited to
sing at a game...and if all goes well I may sing for the Eagles too.

God bless America, land that I love!

CHAPTER 7

A born performer, I loved being in front of the camera. It combined the best of both worlds: writing and being on air. The fast pace, the adrenaline, the camaraderie, the rush of breaking news...I loved the atmosphere even more than being on TV.

My first professional on-air broadcasting opportunity arrived the summer before my senior year, when I did an internship with Suburban Cable in Coatesville, Pennsylvania. Coatesville was very far out on the edges of suburban Philly, a two-hour drive each way from my parents' home twice a week. They produced a weekly thirty-minute newscast, live-to-tape as it was known, focusing on Chester County. As the feature reporter, I would drive to Coatesville, where my twenty-four-year-old boss would assign me a story. Then the photographer and I would take off to wherever the story might be.

I quickly learned how to interview people and put together a "package," as it is called: writing the script, tracking it, doing the stand-up part on camera. I didn't get paid, but it was a real show, and I now had actual tape to give to prospective employers when I graduated.

My senior year of college I researched television stations in media markets all over the country. I couldn't wait to graduate, get out there, and actually work in the field I was so anxious to be part of. I knew exactly how hard it would be to get into that business. I did everything I could to stand out from what was a very crowded pack. I methodically sent hundreds of tapes out, one to every station within a certain radius of my hometown. If I couldn't land a TV job, it would not be for lack of trying.

* * * *

In fourth grade I slacked off a bit, becoming a bit too social, most likely. I came home with a C on my report card for the first—and only—time. It was my first "failure." Not that I was in danger of actually flunking a class or a grade, but I had failed myself, and my parents' expectations. In our discussion of my grades, my father asked if I had truly done my best. I had to admit I hadn't. I'd been lazy, just didn't feel like doing my homework all the time. But the end result was devastating, so not worth it. My parents weren't angry; they were disappointed in me. That was much harder to take.

The second half of fourth grade was much different than the first. My father gave me an assignment book, and I had my teacher sign it every day, ensuring that I brought all my assignments home. My dad signed it every night as well, certifying that I had completed all my homework myself. I appreciated the structure, but I didn't like feeling that my parents no longer trusted me to do the right thing on my own. I would never do this to them again. More importantly, I would never let *myself* down again.

My father always pushed me hard, but I didn't mind. He taught me discipline. When I told him I wanted to be a broadcast journalist, he cautioned me, "That's a tough field. Be prepared to sweep the studio floors at night." I was more than ready to do whatever it took to get a foot in the door. I would sweep whatever, wherever. I went after my first job with that mind-set, and I continue to do so to this very day. Look, if you want something, you have to dedicate yourself to getting it! It's not going to come out of nowhere and drop into your lap. Okay, maybe for a very lucky few...but I never count on luck. I count on myself and hard work.

* * * *

Hard work and that tape from Suburban Cable landed me my first "real" job, my big break. Granted, it was at a tiny cable station in New Jersey. Still, the town where it was situated, Toms River, was part of Ocean County, New Jersey, which surprisingly enough turned out to be a hotbed of news. Melissa Drexler was the teenage girl's name, and she got pregnant. She delivered her baby in a bathroom stall during prom, dumped the live infant in the trash, then returned to the dance floor to party with her boyfriend for the rest of the night. The "Prom Mom" crime riveted the nation, and the national media descended.

Suddenly, I was surrounded by trucks and reporters—big-time, serious people I saw on the national news. Bold-faced marquee reporters, right there in our little neck of the woods. I was in the same crowd, very intimidated, afraid to ask questions. But it was my job. It was the best training imaginable to be forced to step up and hold my own.

A few months later, another national story took center stage. Again, in Ocean County. Eddie Werner, an eleven-year-old Boy Scout in Jackson, New Jersey, was selling candy and wrapping paper door-to-door to raise money for his school. At a house just a few blocks away a teenager opened the door to his knock. Sam Manzie was home alone. He grabbed Eddie by the neck, dragged him inside, and assaulted and strangled him. This was a truly gruesome crime with all kinds of twists and turns. Sam, it turned out, had been repeatedly molested by an older man he met over the internet—a new kind of crime at the time, and a shocking one.

Shortly afterward came a cancer cluster in the area that garnered a great deal of concern from local residents. A number of young children were developing fatal cancers, and no one could figure out why. Activists thought it had something to do with a nuclear power plant in nearby Oyster Creek; they raised a huge fuss and got a lot of media attention. A bunch of celebrities showed up; I got to interview Alec Baldwin and Christie Brinkley, who joined advocating locals.

For such a small station, I was rapidly getting a pretty impressive résumé. I was able to parlay that job into jobs at other stations, and for the rest of my twenties I climbed the ladder. I moved all around: to Champaign, Illinois; a tiny town in Louisiana; News 12 New Jersey; a twenty-four-hour cable network in New Jersey, where I was on camera at Ground Zero the day after the Twin Towers fell. It was all very exciting, everything I had wanted since I was a kid. Truly, I was living the dream. Not that it was easy.

I got turned down for countless jobs I applied for as an anchor. I managed to make my way, but I certainly developed a thick skin. It was like being an actor, constantly auditioning for the next gig. "We don't want another blond." "Not serious enough." "Not pretty enough." "Too pretty." Or just the simple, devastating, "Not good enough." Turndowns were a fact of life. No, no, no, no, no, on down the line. I learned to take all the rejections with a grain of salt, along with criticism. Still, imagine being twenty-three years old and having some cranky viewer in Louisiana calling up to complain, "Your anchor's lips are crooked!" I mean, really? People could be so mean.

My job in Monroe, Louisiana, was actually a great time. Everyone from my station was young and transplanted from all over the country. I quickly acquired a super-cute boyfriend; we had so much fun together. My eyes were certainly opened to a different way of life, what with the Rebel mascot everywhere and a major run-in with the ACLU when local coaches insisted on praying before high school football games.

Shortly after I arrived, while anchoring, I read a news story about a fire at the local mall. Almost anything going on at the Pecanland Mall was a big deal in Monroe. They said that word so oddly in the South: pee-*con*, hitting the second syllable hard. I was from New Jersey, how the hell would I know that; I pronounced it *PE*canland Mall, with the emphasis on the *pee*. Live, on the air. Boy, did those phones light up. The locals were not pleased that I had butchered the name of the mall. The news director took all the calls patiently, then had a word with me. He was nice, but said, "You need to pay attention, learn how people around here talk." Lesson learned.

As a morning anchor, I got up every morning at two a.m. to get ready for work. I had to be constantly ready to move...to wherever the next and best job and market might be. I wasn't married—I barely had time to date!—and didn't have any kids, so I could do it. For a while. I had to be relentlessly single-minded in my pursuit of success, and I was.

CHAPTER 8

For ten years I enjoyed all sorts of adventures. Still, by the time I was nearing thirty I was burning out. In the middle of 2003, I was living in Illinois, where I was the morning anchor for the local NBC affiliate. I had my eye on the big city; we were a feeder market to Chicago, and I had grand ambitions. I had an agent, and we had a plan, one I was working hard to execute. Then I learned that my mother had been diagnosed with breast cancer, and all that didn't seem nearly as urgent or important anymore.

My mom was sick for a time, and I began flying home every weekend, which soon took its toll. I was already exhausted from my regular schedule. On weeknights I was headed for bed at seven p.m., just about the time everyone else was getting ready to go out. I was seriously out of whack with most of my peers, not to mention the wider working world.

Leaving my job was a tough call, but I was spent. I just couldn't keep up the pace anymore. I had worked my butt off for years and had been amply rewarded, but it was time for a change. Don't get me wrong—this decision wasn't nearly as easy as I'm making it sound. A part of me died inside when I left the world of news. It was such a huge part of my identity, but it was time to start a new identity. I lined up a job in my hometown with a prominent PR firm and hoped for the best. Time for the dream to change.

So, there I was, on the verge of thirty and living at home again with my parents. My boss quickly turned out to be the real-life version of Meryl Streep in *The Devil Wears Prada*, only crazier...and meaner. I was far from naïve. I had been a news reporter, which is not an easy business or for those who are sensitive, but this was a whole other level of madness. This woman was absolutely dreadful; each day in that office was a living hell. After only eight intense weeks she did what tornadoes, floods, gruesome accidents, and impossible hours had failed to do: dent my enthusiasm and make me doubt myself. Why had I left a promising broadcasting career to work for such a miserable person?

My sister and I were driving home from a fashion exhibit at the Philadelphia Museum of Art, a welcome break from my horrible schedule. I was unloading on her. I could do PR myself, I told Carolyn. "I am making all the actual bookings for her, and I could certainly call these news people myself and arrange interviews myself. I understand the news business very well, especially from the other side."

"Mindie," my sister said, "sure, you know some people, but there's much more to it than that. How are you going to get clients?"

"I don't know," I said, "but I'm sure it can be done."

"It's not just calling some news contacts or friends you have in the business. There's so much more to being a business owner. It's impossible," she said dismissively. I heard her words, I registered what she was saying, but I didn't let it sink in. I'd noticed, over the years, that many people didn't work hard enough, so they didn't get what they wanted. Then they were disappointed that they didn't get it, assumed they never would, and stopped working hard...a vicious cycle. But not one I would ever fall into. Right or wrong, I always think I can do it. Land some clients? I was sure I could manage it.

That conversation did it; I quit the next day. My finances were in shambles, and I had no idea what to do next, but with my parents' support, I had a little breathing room.

* * * *

I went back to what I knew, taking freelance television jobs in Philly. Small jobs would come in, where I would work a couple days a week for a week or so, maybe. It was not a secure income, and I wasn't really getting anywhere. It was time to make something happen. One afternoon, bored and antsy, I was browsing in a high-end boutique in the suburb of Cherry Hill, New Jersey. The owner was a friendly Jewish woman, the kind who chatted me up and wanted to know all about me and my family.

I told her I had just moved home for a PR job after living all over the country for almost a decade in television news. "But the job didn't work out," I said.

"I'm looking for a publicist," she said. "I just interviewed one in Philadelphia, but I couldn't afford her. How about you help me out, and I'll help you?"

"Oh, I can't make any kind of commitment," I told her. "I don't know where I'm going to be, what's happening work-wise, what I'm doing even next week."

"Honey, it's okay. It's fine, anything you can offer me is great." I had talked big to my sister. Now it was time to walk the talk. I charged her a nominal fee and got to hustling.

There was a chain of stores in the Philadelphia area called Forman Mills, similar to Burlington Coat Factory. The owner's wife happened to be a customer at my new client's store. She saw all the press about the boutique and asked, "How are you all of a sudden everywhere?" the next time she stopped in.

"Oh, I have this great girl, a publicist..." My client put the two of us in touch, the chain of stores became another client... and things just took off from there. I was having my hair cut at the same place I'd been going to since high school, a very trendy salon in suburban Philly. Catching up, the owner asked me what I was up to. I mentioned that I was doing some PR work. "Great," he said. "I could use some PR. What can we work out?"

Suddenly, I had five clients in less than six months. I was making a nice living, and I was enjoying myself. Flying by the seat of my pants...just collecting checks from my clients and cashing them...but I was doing very well. In every area.

A friend of one of my beauty clients had seen me working at their salon one day and liked the look of me; she thought I seemed like a nice girl. She was sure I'd be a good match for her son, a single jeweler named Jason. She arranged for him to show up at the store on a day I was working there. Her plan worked. We met, we talked, he asked me out. We had been dating for a few months, and things were humming right along.

Then, of course, because it's the way life works, out of the blue I got offered a news job. A really good one. It was an anchor position in Scranton, Pennsylvania, a decent-size market just a couple of hours away from Philadelphia. It was a solid offer, but my new boyfriend didn't want me to take it. "I just don't see us being able to maintain a long-distance relationship if you move for that job," he told me. Long distance? I thought he was being a little dramatic.

"I used to fly back and forth from Chicago all the time," I reminded him. "Two hours away is not that big a deal."

"But what about your PR business?" he asked. "You're just going to leave all your clients?" For the first time, I truly realized that I had a business. An actual real, growing concern.

"You have your own business now," he said. "And you're doing great. This can grow. Why would you abandon it?"

Long story short, he convinced me. Being a news anchor was over. Jason and I grew closer and closer. I soon filed the proper papers and formed an official LLC for The Barnett Group and did business as MB and Associates Public Relations. On my thirtieth birthday, everything had turned around. I had my own growing business and a gorgeous engagement ring on my finger. A new life beckoned, and the future was looking bright.

Power Passage # 3

PUT YOUR BEST FOOT FORWARD

"You can have anything you want in life if you dress for it."

—EDITH HEAD

Wearing just the right outfit makes me feel pretty and happy... and who doesn't want that? It started way back in fourth or fifth grade, with Esprit and Forenza and all the other trendy brands of the time. In high school I was always dressed to the nines. I would carefully prepare each day for school with meticulously planned outfits; I also wore fancy hats to match my winter coats. I never wore the same coat two days in a row, either; I had six or seven that I switched out. My absolute favorite was a red swing coat with bell sleeves and wide black trim around the bottom, with big black buttons. I think it came from the Limited clothing store. With it I wore a red fedora with black satin trim and a bow in the back. It was fabulous!

As a senior in high school, I would park in the senior lot in the morning and then saunter across the football field, carrying my satchel like I was on a runway. My BFF, Heather, and I always wore adorable outfits, every day; we were known for it. When I went to college, students were much more casual. They dressed down quite a lot. I never did that, though of course I did the leggings thing. When I got into TV, I had to wear suits, but I made sure they were always to die for. Even if I had to skip a meal—literally. I spent most of my money on clothes! A ridiculous percentage of my paychecks went straight to shoes and clothes, period. My habit made me happy. If I looked in the mirror and liked what I saw, it made for a much better start to the day. And there is no price tag too high for that!

Moving forward, after I got out of news and into public relations, I started representing some incredible fashion leaders. Not only was I an avid consumer, but I now started to get a real education on the business. I attended trade shows and fashion shows in New York City, learned how buyers at boutiques worked, began to understand seasonal trends and design lines. I was mesmerized by every aspect of the business. The way concepts by designers like Chanel and Hermes and Gucci trickle down to average consumers through Target or Macy's was fascinating to me. The whole concept of the current "color," announced by the Pantone Institute every year, was very interesting; it also segued to so many things in everyday life. I could write and pitch all kinds of trend pieces about one color for my fashion clients or hair or home décor. How to spruce up your home with teal accents, for example.

On the side, I started freelance writing for *South Jersey Magazine* and some other regional publications...to keep honing my writing skills. Writing for print was much more difficult than writing for television, and I needed to keep my skills sharp. One day I was out on a fashion shoot, and I was appalled at the selection of clothes. "Is that what you're using?" I asked the editor. It was all just so wrong; the pieces looked like someone just grabbed them out of the store with no thought. Nothing blended together; there was no coherent theme or story line. It was a bunch of random things. It was dreadful!

"What do you think?" the editor asked me, and I immediately made several suggestions. By the end of our talk, she asked, "Would you like to be our stylist?" I accepted on the spot. From that point on, I was the stylist for any fashion shoots, which usually came in the fall, for winter holidays, Valentine's Day jewelry, spring trends, and summer swimsuits. Sometimes I went to certain stores we patronized because they were big advertisers; other times I went to my own picks. I would take a photo and the measurements of the models with me and go pull clothes for each of them. I would then schlep to the shoot with all the clothes, separated by model, and outfit each person to make sure they were dressed impeccably. I remember a particular shoot on the beach at Cape May, New Jersey, that included an overnight stay. We worked so many hours! I was eight months pregnant doing that gig, in the scorching sun, sweating…. I touched my belly and said, "We're having so much fun, Arielle! You're at a fashion shoot with Mommy and you don't even know it!"

* * * *

I never went to school for fashion. It's all self-taught; I just have a knack. I've been "dressing" my friends since grade school. I'm always accompanying someone shopping. When I worked in news I jumped at all the fashion and lifestyle segments, everything from the best handbags for spring to how to wear white after Labor Day to how to dress for your body type. I was also great at "ambush makeovers," where I'd take a local woman out and shop with them, pick out the most flattering outfit for them, and oversee their hair and makeup. This passion goes for men too—I always enjoyed picking out clothes for boyfriends or my husband or even my cousin Jeremy.

New York, of course, is a fantastic shopping destination. I particularly love the Flatiron district and Madison Avenue, with all its unique boutiques. I much prefer boutiques over big stores; I never want to look too much like everybody else. I like a touch of the unusual. Bohemian is my favorite look; Rachel Zoe is my fashion idol. I love her style. Actually, there's nothing I don't love about that woman. Saks does have a boutique vibe.... Nordstrom's has a great active line. With Saks and boutiques, you can't go wrong. Then there are shoes. As someone who devoted an entire half basement in a large family home to house her shoe collection along with her overflowing amount of apparel, I have very strong feelings about shoes.

The Shoe Box in New York is amazing, with super-trendy, fun styles, and more affordable than Prada or Gucci. Not inexpensive by any means, but not obscene. I recently discovered Schutz Shoes near Barneys, which stocks the most gorgeous shoes ever. To this day I still wear my favorite pair of shoes: gold sparkly sandals from Head Start Shoes in Philadelphia. I wear them out with flare jeans, ripped shorts, or shift dresses. Being five-foot-two means always hemming your pants...always...and I have a system. When I buy bell-bottoms, I usually get them hemmed in one of two lengths: shorter or longer, depending on the shoe. Heels or flats. With these particular sandals I wear the pants hemmed for flats, so they peek out. A little bling goes a long way! When I walk, you can appreciate the whole shoe. As you can see, I devote a lot of thought to this kind of thing.

What can I say? As Carrie Bradshaw once said, "I like my money right where I can see it—hanging in my closet." She is one smart woman! These days I direct much of my fashion energy to Instagram. Check it out at @mindie.barnett. And never underestimate the power of looking your best!

CHAPTER 9

My clock was already ticking when I got married, because Jason and I hoped to have more than one child. We had a great townhome in Marlton, New Jersey, near Philadelphia; my business was doing well; we were already in our thirties. There was no time to waste; I was absolutely yearning for a baby. To celebrate our first year of marriage we took a Mediterranean cruise through Europe. Before we left, I tossed my birth control pills. I could not have been more excited; I was sure I would get pregnant right away. Hopefully on our anniversary trip.

Growing up, my sister, Carolyn, had suffered from endometriosis, and doctors had warned her since adolescence that she might have a hard time conceiving. For years she'd been asking—jokingly, but with serious undertones—"Please, will you be my surrogate if I need one?" "Of course," was my answer, without hesitation. Absolutely I would. The possibility of having difficulty conceiving was very much on her mind all her life. I, on the other hand, had no such issues or worries. Actually trying to get pregnant, after years of trying to avoid it, was quite a switch.

Several months passed, with plenty of passionate sex, which was fantastic, because it brought my husband and me much closer. We had a shared purpose, and we were happily working on our common goal. Six months later, my sister, who had recently married, announced that she was pregnant. Anticipating a long wait, they'd started "trying" right away. She conceived shortly after her honeymoon...with the ease I thought I would have but didn't. I was delighted for my sister, of course, but getting a tiny bit concerned about myself. Still, everyone said to give it a year.

At the gynecologist's office for a routine checkup, I saw the doctor my sister and I had been seeing all our lives. Conversation naturally turned to her big news. "I'm trying too," I said. "But it doesn't seem to be happening. I wonder if I should get tested." I was just about to turn thirty-four. I knew thirty-five was the age of caution.

"Your age is right on the borderline of when we suggest some sort of treatment after six months of trying. But yes, I would say you should go ahead and see an infertility doctor, just to be safe," Dr. Wu said. That was the first time I heard that word applied to me. Infertile? Seeing the look on my face, she rushed to reassure me. "It might not have anything to do with you; there could be an issue with your husband. Or it might not be anything at all. It can't hurt to just go and get checked." She recommended a specialist, whom I went to see immediately.

After taking ten full vials of blood from my arm, they had enough to check for anything and everything. Jason's sperm was also tested, but they concentrated much more on me and how every one of my bits was functioning. All my test results came back perfectly normal. Jason's sperm were apparently strong swimmers, so any issues we were having were termed "unexplained." This was a catchall phrase, I learned: "unexplained infertility." It was time to "try harder."

How to track my ovulation was explained to me and I started peeing on a stick every morning to monitor my hormones. From that point on, we had sex on a schedule. The ideal time for intercourse was on the day of ovulation. We weren't allowed to spontaneously just "do it" anymore, because Jason's sperm needed to be built up, apparently. It became that tiresome scene where we'd both be exhausted after long days at work and I'd say, "We have to have sex tonight." What had started so joyously was becoming a grim chore.

In addition to tracking my ovulation myself, I was monitored every morning at the doctor's office during that one critical week each month. Based on my hormone levels, I might or might not be given a vaginal ultrasound that day. Each night I got an official call directing me to either have sex that night or return in the morning. After the optimum day for sex, it was time to wait. I would then return for a pregnancy test, and they'd call to let me know if I had conceived or not.

I got used to trekking into Jefferson Hospital in Philadelphia all the time, a long haul at six thirty in the morning. Sitting in that waiting room was so depressing. I was surrounded by women in their thirties and forties, absolutely desperate to become mothers. Their sadness and strain were evident on their faces. And there I was, equally desperate, equally anxious. For the next few months, I got a call from the nurse, very matter-of-fact. "You are negative," she would say.

I was becoming a little panicky. My sister was about to deliver. My best friend, Ali, after a heartbreaking miscarriage, was also expecting again, this time enjoying a healthy, successful pregnancy. Everywhere I looked, everyone was pregnant or with their baby. Everyone but me. After a lifetime of good health, I couldn't believe it. I was a good eater. I maintained a strict exercise regimen. What was wrong with me?

The next step was Clomid, a drug that stimulated my system to over-ovulate, basically. The more eggs produced, the better the odds that I'd get pregnant, in a nutshell. I got through one round, as they called it, but suffered every possible side effect, so we moved on to the next treatment. That was gonadotropins, which also overstimulated my ovaries, working on them directly through daily injections. This was an even more potent treatment than Clomid. To no avail, as several more months passed with no good news.

Then we tried IUI, intrauterine insemination, which meant artificially inseminating me with Jason's sperm as I lay there, then held my legs high up in the air for half an hour, hoping it would take. With IUI, we were no longer having actual sex at all, as the process was done remotely, as it were. The various treatments caused my ovaries to swell to the size of grapefruits every month. My stomach stuck out grotesquely on my five-foot-two-inch frame. It was so noticeable that several acquaintances congratulated me on what appeared to be my pregnancy, adding insult to injury. My periods were more like hemorrhaging. The whole process was hard on me, body and soul. It was a long three months and yet again, no happy news. It was time for the big guns: in vitro fertilization, or IVF.

CHAPTER 10

learned slowly but surely along my journey that a lot of women are not particularly anxious to share their stories about struggling to conceive. Though infertility is very common, many who suffer through it have no desire to discuss it; it's a very private, loaded subject. A woman I knew casually had had twins; a mutual friend told me that she'd had IVF. I wanted to hear her success story, so the next time I saw her at the gym I made a point of chatting with her. I inquired about her twins, now a year old, and I told her I was having a really hard time getting pregnant. She asked me a few questions, then said, "You should see Dr. Check. He's not your regular MD—more like a mad scientist—but he's the best." I assumed he must have been the doctor who treated her, but she didn't share any details and I didn't press her. I just thanked her for the referral.

Dr. Check was an unusual man. I'd been seeing quite a few doctors over the past year, and he definitely stood out from the rest. For one, he was world renowned. Why this man chose Marlton, New Jersey, for his practice, I can't say, as he was an international authority on infertility issues. He had patients flying in to see him from across the globe. His office was full of antique furniture and incense was burning, not your standard clinical setting at all. After our first appointment he sent me home with stacks of medical studies he had authored. I was all for science, but I wasn't looking to get a PhD; I just wanted a baby. How he managed that was his business. "I'm not so sure about this," I told Jason. Turned out it was far from the only problem.

Up until this point, our health insurance had covered these various treatments. We learned that IVF would not be covered, at all. IVF is a very expensive procedure, ten thousand dollars a procedure, at least. With IUI, they were trying to produce two or three viable eggs; with IFV, the goal was eight. I already knew in my bones I was going to have massive issues with this latest treatment, as my body had reacted so poorly to the others. Now we had to worry about affording it, as the doctors recommended at least two rounds. There was no guarantee of it taking the first time. The success rate for IUI was 25 percent; for IVF it was closer to 50 percent. So, we looked into taking out a second mortgage. We were willing to do what it took...whatever it took.

For in vitro fertilization, very simply, intact eggs are collected and screened, put into a petri dish, inseminated with healthy sperm, then implanted back inside the uterus. Not all eight eggs, of course. As I was doing my research I learned about the possibility of becoming an egg donor. I found out that many women become egg donors because the woman receiving the egg(s) would pay for a round of IVF, since they were unable to produce their own. As an egg donor, half the number of eggs I would produce on my round—let's say eight total—four would go to her, and four would go to me. These women would be inseminated with their own partner's sperm and my egg, then hopefully carry the pregnancy to fruition.

Some people found it a bit strange or off-putting that there might be another child in the world somewhere that was genetically related to them but never known, but I looked at it another way. As badly as I was suffering, I knew there were plenty of women out there who had it worse. Many couldn't even produce eggs; I could at least do that. Maybe this was a way to help someone in a terrible situation. To allow both of us to have the baby we longed for. Jason was a little put off by the whole idea, but he eventually came around.

We also started thinking about adoption. Jason wasn't quite ready to throw in the towel, but my body was rebelling. Physically, but also emotionally. Every time I got the bad news—the phone call saying it hadn't worked this month either—I cried for days. I became extremely emotional; all the hormones didn't help. My sister had her baby, so did Ali. I was elated for them, sad for myself. The conflicting emotions of joy, sorrow, and increasing panic were hard to handle.

I didn't get everything in life I had set out to; no one ever does. But I had always been a firm believer in setting goals, trying my hardest, working relentlessly, and refusing to give up while hoping for the best. Nothing had ever shaken my faith in myself and my innate optimism. I had always felt in control of my own destiny. The realization that I might not be able to perform such a primal function—giving birth, raising a family—was a big wake-up call saying I was not in charge of everything. Or maybe anything at all. I went to synagogue. "Please God, make me a mom," I prayed every week, fervently. But I also hedged my bets.

I met with an adoption lawyer and researched the pros and cons of domestic and international adoption. I learned that the trend in domestic adoptions nowadays was very much toward open adoptions, where the birth parents often stay quite involved in the child's life. I wasn't sure I could handle that kind of shared parental relationship. I wanted a baby, my own baby, so desperately. I decided that if it came down to it, I would absolutely adopt internationally, hopefully giving him or her a better life. But first, I would try IVF.

* * * *

If we had the resources to do only two rounds, we were going to go to the best. I returned to Dr. Check's office, where I was put in the care of Dr. Brazille, under Dr. Check's supervision. He wanted to run his own set of tests again...so off we went with the ten vials, all the tests, déjà vu. I was not pleased. When he called us in to go over the results, he said, "I want you to do a couple more rounds of IUI."

"Absolutely not. I don't want to do it; it's too hard on my body. It didn't work, either time," I said immediately.

He explained that he had discovered that Jason had some sort of anomaly in his sperm. Though healthy and strong, a very small portion of antibodies were present, likely inhibiting the sperm from implanting on the egg. The doctor had a plan. He advised that the sperm be "washed" with a solution to destroy these antibodies. "All we need to do is get the antibodies off these sperm, and I am pretty confident this will work out," he said. He pushed us hard to agree to two more rounds of IUI.

Very reluctantly I agreed to one more round. If that didn't work, we were moving on to IVF. Frankly, I thought we were wasting time. I went in, got the sperm injections, kept my legs in the air, the whole time thinking, *This isn't going to work.* I drove home and put it out of my head. The next week I felt strange.

I felt crampy, my breasts hurt, my sinuses ached.... Something was off. I went in for my blood test, as usual, thinking, *Could it be?* Oddly, I didn't get my regular end-of-workday call that night, which made both Jason and me very antsy. We figured if it was good news, they'd be in a hurry to share it.

Finally, at about eight p.m., the phone rang. "Mindie, you tested positive," the nurse told me. Jason came over to hug me; we both cried tears of relief, called our parents, celebrated. It was such a happy night. Then all I had to do was worry about pregnancy! I stayed at the same clinic for my care for the first trimester, as they liked to monitor "their" pregnancies. I got to switch sides. I literally moved from one side of the waiting room to the other, and I stood in a different line for tests. I was in the "pregnant" line now, and it was very hard for me to see the naked pain and envy in the eyes of the other women still trying as they glanced in my direction. All this made quite an impression on type A, control freak me. This journey was a great lesson that *I was not in charge of everything*, one I vowed to keep in mind in the future.

CHAPTER 11

I t is a Jewish tradition to name a child after a deceased family member to honor them and keep their memory alive via the new life. The name itself might be the ancestor's Hebrew name, their middle name, their first name...and it doesn't even have to be their actual name. Anything with the same first initial is fine. I wanted to name our first child for my beloved Pop-Pop Al, and Jason was fine with that. We were on a trip to Disneyworld, alone, on what turned out to be our last visit without kids. We strolled around the park, leisurely discussing possibilities that started with the letter *A*.

At that time, we were surrounded by Avas. We met a new baby Ava every time we turned around, so that was out. At the end of that mild early-summer day, we stayed to watch the famous electrical parade. And when I got a glimpse of the Little Mermaid float going by, a light bulb went off in my head. Watching the beautiful Ariel, I said, "Oh, Ariel, that's an *A*! Jason, what do you think of Ariel for a girl?" He agreed, so we decided to name our daughter-to-be Arielle, spelled in the French way, with the emphasis on the *elle*. Her middle name was also a breeze—once the first part was chosen, we swiftly opted for Rose, in honor of Jason's deceased grandmother. With that settled, we furnished the nursery, prepared for the birth, and worked even harder.

Only six months after starting my business with my first retail client, I had rented office space in Center City, Philadelphia, hired an assistant, and never looked back. At this time, I currently had an office in Haddonfield, New Jersey, three full-time staff members, and a number of demanding clients. Business was great; by the time I got pregnant, MB and Associates Public Relations had officially been going strong for more than four years.

Ideally, I would have loved to scale back once I had a baby, just keep a few key clients and work mostly from home. However, just about the time Arielle was scheduled to arrive, Jason left the company he worked for and went out on his own with a fine-jewelry and diamond business. This ultimately turned out to be a great move on his part, but in the beginning, there was no chance of my cutting back. We had a mortgage, a condo at the Jersey shore, and a baby on the way. We needed both incomes, so I had to keep on charging, which fortunately was not too difficult for me. In short, I did what I had to do, like most moms!

My due date was July 22, and I decided to take off a few days before and the week after the birth, as well. At a checkup in early July, I wasn't even slightly dilated; the doctor kept saying he thought he would eventually have to induce labor because I wasn't nearly far enough along. I returned home for a long wait, resigning myself to the fact that this baby would arrive late. Instead, she showed up ten days early, in the middle of the night!

I could not have been more surprised at three a.m. when I felt a big kick and my water broke. All of a sudden, birth was upon me, and I was not ready! I had my whole week overscheduled. I was that woman you see in labor on her cell phone with the office. It was ridiculous; my husband was not happy with me. Arielle was born on a Wednesday, we brought her home, and I was back at work bright and early Monday morning. I was breastfeeding and banging away on my computer keyboard all day long...happily so. Having my beautiful baby gave me super strength and power to tackle work and motherhood. Just one look at that precious face, and I knew I was not going to let her down. Ever. I was going to do it all!

* * * *

I breastfed Arielle every couple of hours. At night, I would take her out of the bassinet at my side, sit propped up against a pillow, and get her securely latched on. As I sat there in a half-dozed state, I would tell myself that I was on an airplane, flying first class, en route on the red-eye for a work meeting. An hour later I would switch sides and doze as Arielle nursed for another hour. She would be awake and hungry again two hours later. This scenario went on all night...until six thirty a.m., at which point I had to get out of bed and prepare for a long day.

I lived on caffeine and Red Bull...the approved amounts, of course, whatever I was allowed to have while breastfeeding. My news background—jumping up in the middle of the night, getting no sleep, being under the gun—all came in very handy. Those first few months were tough; I can't deny it. Work didn't slow down because I'd had a baby!

I not only worked *in* downtown Haddonfield, where I had my office, but I worked *with* it as well. The Partnership for Haddonfield, as it was known, was a great client; they had been with me for a couple of years and it was a terrific relationship on both sides. I had gotten the group some great coverage and press; the director was happy with my work. However, after two years they had to open the account for bids from everyone; this was the system protocol for all nonprofit government bodies. I was assured it was just a formality and I would retain the job, but other PR firms had to at least be considered.

The application process to represent a nonprofit government agency was, naturally, extremely complicated. The forms were so involved, so extensive, so full of nitpicky details that it took days to complete everything. I worked on it feverishly to meet the deadline, even working after temple on the day of Rosh Hashanah to get it done. I had the whole thing finished, double-checked, bound, and ready to go. I brought the application portfolio in with me to my office and put it in a prominent place on my desk with a sigh of relief, ready to turn it in the next day.

I was sitting quietly, just catching up on emails late that afternoon, when the phone rang. It was the director of the Partnership. "Mindie, where are you?" she asked. "The application is due today. We must have it by five p.m." My heart nearly jumped out of my chest. I couldn't believe it. I had gotten confused on the date, something I prided myself on never doing. Per the rules, the application had to be dropped off in person and not emailed. I grabbed it and literally raced the three blocks, weaving in and out of traffic, to the municipal office, where members of the board were all gathered. I missed the deadline by five minutes. I also lost the account. It was so dumb! It was new-mom brain. I was so angry with myself; this was a real setback. I was a bit shaken going home that night. This was going to be harder than I had thought.

And so began the endless teeter-totter of the working mom. PR is all about networking and making contacts and keeping up with journalists and bloggers and influencers. Most of these gatherings took place at happy hours, or at night, when I wanted to be home with my baby.

I was with Arielle as much as possible, but sometimes, on hard days, I had the sinking feeling that even while I was with her, I wasn't 100 percent present, if only because I was always working so hard. I was physically present, but my mind was on the next business meeting, the press release I had to write, the TV show I wanted to book. Then at work I'd worry about my baby and how she was faring without me. It was that divided feeling all moms have; I just had to power through and trust I was doing the best I could do on both fronts.

Power Passage #4

START A BRAG BOOK

> "Our deepest fear is not that we are inadequate. Our deepest fear is that we are powerful beyond measure. It is our light, not our darkness, that most frightens us. We ask ourselves, 'Who am I to be brilliant, gorgeous, talented, fabulous?' Actually, who are you not to be? You are a child of God. Your playing small does not serve the world."
>
> —MARIANNE WILLIAMSON, *A Return to Love*

Actress Amy Schumer, in an interview about her film *I Feel Pretty*, said something along the lines of "I feel great about myself. When I look into the mirror I do see a supermodel. My parents raised me to think I really was the smartest, funniest, prettiest girl ever. I feel that way today." I think that's a great attitude not only for her, but for all women! I also think I'm awesome, and I deserve all good things. I want everyone who reads this book to feel good about themselves and deserving of all that it is they want. We all have something special to bring to the table. Let's stop being so down on ourselves for what we aren't, and celebrate what we are!

It's hard to do it all, especially when we want to do everything perfectly. We strive to be super-wife, super-mom, super-employee; we want everything to go just right, while looking good, remaining calm, and juggling a hundred balls. That's just not realistic. Work is not fair.... Life is not fair. There are days you will get in trouble when it's not your fault, things that go wrong that are out of your control. There will always be someone who is disappointed in your performance or choices, whatever it is you've done. Like many women, I always want everyone to be happy with me. But in the PR business, let's get real. You can't please a wacko. Some clients are just impossible, and some of the stuff they throw at me is not really about me. I accept the blame, don't argue uselessly when there's nothing to be won, and move on to the next thing!

This attitude didn't happen overnight. Over the course of my career I've had plenty of minor mishaps along the way. A client got an email once with an egregious spelling mistake. It was just a pitch to a reporter, but it got forwarded directly on to the proposed subject, the head of a hospital. This man read the pitch and called me directly to point out what was, in the end, really just a typo. It was humiliating. I dwelled on this small mistake endlessly; this incident haunted me for weeks. Yes, I should have caught it, but I was far more remorseful than I should have been. I think it's very easy to fall prey to this kind of thinking, and it's important to guard against it. I care a great deal about my work...which is a good trait. But, like many women, I take criticism to heart more than I should, which is a not-so-good trait.

In a *Wall Street Journal* article about women and self-confidence, career coach Aimee Cohen suggested to a client that she start a "brag book"—a journal for saving notes about one's accomplishments, to aid recall of "rock-star moments." I thought this was a fantastic idea, and one I took advantage of. There's so much out there about gratitude and counting one's blessings, and I'm certainly all for that. I know some people who have a journal and write down something to be grateful for every day. So why not a brag book, something to remind yourself every day how truly amazing you really are?

I was already in the habit of using a version of this trick on bad days as I drove home from the office. I'd put whatever happened that day out of my mind—I'd already spent sufficient time analyzing it—and focus on remembering achievements from the past: when I landed my biggest account, when I booked a client on a national program, when my company won a prestigious award. Reliving a win lifts spirits; there's no doubt about it. A brag book serves the same purpose as a tangible reminder of your "biggest hits."

With the right mind-set and confidence level, the world is your oyster. It is the most important thing in the world to continually remind yourself of just what you are capable of... not in the past, not as a fluke, but every day, now and in the future to come.

CHAPTER 12

knew very well how much I owed to all the mentors I have had in my life, and I kept that firmly in mind whenever someone reached out to me. I particularly gravitated toward students who had just graduated, or women looking to transition into other careers; I always did my best to help them out and try to offer helpful advice and direction. It was only good karma.

So, I was delighted one day when an old friend got in touch. This woman—let's call her Jane Doe—and I had worked at a news station together back in the day. I had known her since my second year in the business. We stayed in touch in the ensuing years; I considered her a dear friend. We were really close. When I married Jason, she was one of my bridesmaids. She had recently lost her job...for a very good reason, I would come to find out, but at the time I didn't question it at all. I just knew she was at loose ends. Looking for work, needing a hand.

I had just lost an associate who was moving when Jane came to me and said, "How about I help you and you help me?" I agreed, mainly because I thought it would be a short-term solution for us both. I never figured she would stay long, because this girl had a healthy ego. She didn't just like the spotlight;

she lived for the camera. Don't get me wrong, I like it too, but it isn't my reason for being. I had long since adjusted to a job behind the scenes, promoting others. I thought our arrangement might last for six months, a year tops.

It was never a great match, work-wise, but because of our long history, I cut her some slack. Too much slack, as I was a little too grateful to have a "peer" in the office. She did a number of questionable things over the years she stayed, which was always quite awkward as she was my friend as well as an employee and I hesitated to reprimand her. When she did something really wildly inappropriate in front of a client, I finally had to confront her. She had become more than a problem. Still, I made the parting gentle. I "laid her off." Then I found out what a liability she truly was!

I had her work emails forwarded to me from the office computer she used, standard office protocol. I read some puzzling emails from a reporter we worked with, going back and forth about a shoot I knew nothing about. I called Jane to find out what this was about and she quickly came up with some lie...and I knew something was off. This triggered a full-scale investigation. I soon discovered contracts for representation in her name on her work computer in addition to hundreds and hundreds of emails doing her own business, going back a couple of years. She had been running her own business, on my time! And using my company name when reaching out to the media.

I came to find out she was actually signing and representing clients, giving out my office rollover line and answering them with her own name in tandem with my company name.... Jane Doe Public Relations, she likely sang out in the middle of my office, while sending out all kinds of correspondence under that name. She had more than a few clients, all of whom she tried to take with her when we parted ways. To think, I had been willing to let her go quietly. I had planned to give her severance pay, help her find other work to do, pay her for unused vacation days…. It would be my little mitzvah, a small good deed, quietly done, simply to be a good person. But now, oh *hell* no. It killed me just to hand over her last paycheck as required by law.

The more I dug into this whole affair, the more I felt like I was starring in a Lifetime movie about the crazy friend who takes over your business or life. We never spoke again, not directly, but I did wind up suing her. In the course of legal discovery I learned she was still doing PR, with her adult daughter as her partner. The adult daughter not one friend had ever known she had!

My mind flashed back to the sad time when I was having infertility issues. I used to literally cry on her shoulder about my situation. At any one of those many moments she could have chimed in with, "I understand. I'm a mom too." How do you just sit there and listen like you don't understand what it is to want to have kids? How did I have a friend, one I'd vacationed with, partied with, known since we were kids practically, not tell me about her own kid? Had I ever even known her? Apparently not!

It was all so strange. That was such a stressful time in my business; I felt very put upon, more hurt than anything. I was so utterly blindsided. I trusted Jane; I was so good to her. I lent her a car when she needed one. I gave her bonuses, presents; we shared Thanksgiving holidays at my parents' home. Just thinking of the full-time salary I had paid that woman, for years, while she was concentrating on building her own business on my resources the entire time was infuriating! The risk she put me in, if something had gone wrong on one of "her" shoots. It made my blood run cold just to think of it. It was a major betrayal.

This incident really opened my eyes to what "friends" are capable of, that's for sure. It was another good life lesson, a business one, a tough one. Everyone in town was talking about it; we were the mini scandal in the local news world. In fact, the whole mess wound up in the papers. Because I pitched it! It was well within my rights; court issues were a matter of public record. The sordid little affair wound up in the gossip section of *The Philadelphia Inquirer* and *Philadelphia Daily News*. Don't mess with a publicist, is the lesson there! Or someone who used to be an investigative reporter. I am a nice person, but not a pushover! I am strong, and I will fight when wronged. If you are going to screw me, you're going to get it back! With a vengeance.

CHAPTER 13

I had certainly not forgotten what it had taken to get our precious Arielle. I figured we would have to go through all that "infertility" rigamarole again, should we ever want to expand our family. Particularly because I would now officially be what was called a "high-risk pregnancy," due to my age. For the moment, I wasn't thinking about it. I was a typical frantic working mom. I had only recently potty-trained Arielle and was thrilled to finally return to my regular workout schedule.

One night I felt a strange yet oddly familiar flulike feeling. I felt like I was coming down with something. Crampy, sore, and painful breasts. For a second the possibility of pregnancy flashed through my mind, but I immediately dismissed it. Sex was not a frequent thing, with our two growing businesses and one toddler. There was no way; in fact, I had just had a few drinks the week before, at a client's restaurant opening, a rare treat I would not have dreamed of indulging in if we were "trying." I figured I was coming down with something and I headed out to the drugstore for some medicine. A monster of a snowstorm was on the way, and I didn't want to get stuck inside the house, sick, with no medicine.

I threw Nyquil and sinus medicine in my basket, then, in an overabundance of caution, tossed in the cheapest pregnancy test I could find. That sort of medication was strictly forbidden if pregnant, and I was nothing if not careful. I entered the guest bathroom upstairs as soon as I got home and took the test, anxious to get some medicine in my system. When I saw that the stick result was positive, I was thunderstruck. I sat in the bathroom just staring at it for a long time. Then I called my mom. I had not even thought to first tell Jason. "Mom," I said in between sobs, "I'm pregnant! I'm so upset. I'm not ready for this."

"This is a good thing, Mindie," my mom said, trying to talk me off the ledge. "Everything will be fine. This is exciting news!"

Next, I ran to tell Jason, who was showering in our bathroom, down the hall. "Jason!" I screamed. "Open the door!" Impatient, I knocked on the door in a panic, and as he pulled it open I thrust the stick in his face.

"What the hell is that?" he asked, confused. Then it dawned on him. "No way, that can't be right."

"I know, it can't. Can you go back out to the store for another test?" He came home with three high-end, expensive tests and I took them all. All three were positive. Seven months later, along came our son, Julian, named for Jason's Uncle Jay who had passed away. He was the biggest surprise of my life. People say, once you've been pregnant, you're much more fertile, that the body wants to get pregnant again. I'll say!

* * * *

Come fall, I had tried to prepare for some sort of leave. I was due October 1. The timing prior wasn't ideal. I was in the middle of one of my biggest projects yet: Philadelphia's Fashion Week, and my PR firm was heavily involved. This kind of event was a big deal for Philly, and a plum project for my firm and one of our clients who was to be featured a great deal on The Red Carpet. As it was still in its infancy, there was only a minor blueprint to follow. I had to be on top of every last detail, personally involved with literally every single decision associated with my client.

Naturally, Julian arrived three weeks early, only days before the September event date. I was literally once again talking on my cell phone as they were wheeling me to the labor room. Jason couldn't believe it. "You're not a surgeon! You're not saving the world! Nothing is that important, give me that phone!"

We had moved into our dream house in Mount Laurel, New Jersey, by the time Julian was born. All I wanted to do was wheel my beautiful new baby around our breathtaking new neighborhood in his carriage on the brisk autumn days after his birth. It sounds crazy, but I simply could not physically get out the door with him. I could not manage to get off that phone or computer or conference call or FaceTime or whatever one of the thousand and one things that kept me chained to my desk in my home office. I watched our nanny wheel him out the door and head off down the road, as I waved from my window. I was on the phone, standing and watching in a daze, as they disappeared around the corner. I felt a deep pang of regret as I really wanted to be the one pushing my baby. I knew these were bonding experiences I would never get back.

Our new home had its own finished basement. The realtor had called it a mother-in-law suite; our nanny lived there five nights a week. Tina was with me for the first year of Julian's life. She lived with us during the week and went home to Connecticut on weekends, which eventually became too much of a commute given the weather in the Northeast and transportation. We parted ways very amicably; she went on to have a baby and we stayed friendly. I was then fortunate to find Alicia, who has been with us ever since and is now part of the family. She was simply amazing. She kept the same schedule; she lived in five days and went home to Philly on weekends.

I could never have done what I did without their help. As the owner of a PR firm, there were countless functions every night of the week I "should" have gone to. Business opportunities I missed. I made sure my office was represented, but of course that wasn't the same as being there myself. I could always have been doing more, on both fronts. I'm not going to lie...I missed some moments. I was not one of those moms who could sit on the sidelines watching every one of Arielle's gymnastics practices, though I would have loved to. Again, I kept it moving, and things were working for me, but honestly, I think I just had a naturally high threshold for stress and lack of sleep.

In hindsight, I was lucky that I had to work; my business kept growing and would later allow me the financial independence to leave my marriage, something I may not have had if I had cut back and stayed home. What's the old saying.... You make plans, God laughs?

* * * *

So many marriages run into serious problems once kids come along because the woman doesn't want to have sex anymore; often because she's too busy, tired, or preoccupied with the kids. I knew all about this common complaint. I'd heard about it from both sides, male and female friends. I had the opposite problem. There was nothing I wanted more in my marriage than passion, connection, romance, sparks. My husband, unfortunately, wasn't as interested as I was.

I'd made our beautiful master bathroom sanctuary as inviting as possible. The large space was divided into sections, with the toilet and shower hidden behind closed doors. The dramatic tub was the showpiece of the main room, which you had to walk through to reach the toilet or shower. More than a few nights I would be taking a bath and Jason would walk in to use the bathroom. He wouldn't even glance over at me as he passed by. This cut me to the core of my being. Jason would go in and leave. I would sit in the tub and cry, feeling unattractive, and unlovable, and like absolute shit.

When Julian was about six months old, Jason and I were attending a wedding. It was on a Friday night, and we arranged for the kids to sleep at my parents' because we were going to stay out so late. I made a big effort. I had a pretty dress to wear, but underneath I put on some sexy lingerie, including a black lace bustier. I sat at my makeup table in our bedroom as we dressed for the affair, posing there right in front of my husband in that sexy lingerie, and he didn't even mention it. I don't think he did it on purpose; it wasn't to hurt my feelings, but I did not feel desired or attractive. I hadn't for a very long time.

I went into my closet for a brief but intense crying session before finally drying my eyes and coming out. I redid my makeup, put on my beautiful dress, and headed to Jason's shiny Infiniti sedan, where he courteously held the door open for me. We went to his cousin's wedding. It all looked good on the outside. Inside was a different story.

Power Passage #5

SEEK GUIDANCE EVERYWHERE

"There is no death, only a change of worlds."

—CHIEF SEATTLE

As I scrolled through my social media, a shout-out to Meghan Markle—the world's most famous newlywed and popular princess—caught my eye. A makeup artist thanked her for recommending a "truly gifted" intuitive, one he claimed was "the real deal," who had helped him bring one of his most long-standing dreams to fruition. This post, of course, led to much speculation that Meghan, like Princess Diana before her, has sought out "the other side" for guidance and solace. Like an estimated 25 percent of American women who look to the other side for answers, I find myself in good company!

I've always had an interest in otherworldly phenomena. I've visited mediums several times in my life; psychics and intuitive readings were always something I was very open to. Whenever I was facing the unknown and looking for answers, I was willing to look to wherever they might come from. Well, not so much answers, maybe, as reassurance. No one goes to see a psychic or healer when everything's going great. I was looking for someone to tell me everything was going to be okay in the end, that everything was going to be all right. I generally asked about the usual concerns: boyfriends and jobs when I was younger; my kids and my health when I got older.

This is not to say I disregarded the more traditional avenues for help with a troubled marriage. I was unhappy, getting steadily unhappier, and stuck. I couldn't seem to find a way out, so I entered therapy with one concrete goal in mind: to tell my husband that I wanted a divorce. This wasn't my first rodeo; my husband and I, like many couples, had tried marriage counseling at one point. However, it quickly became clear that the relationship was no longer viable. I soon decided I needed to continue going to therapy for me.

My first therapist was empathetic and agreed with everything I said. She was very affirming to me, and in several of our discussions—about change, for example—she gave me some good, solid guidance. She was just what I needed at that point: somebody basically to vent to and tell me that my feelings were valid. I wasn't looking so much for advice about what to do in that sense; it was becoming increasingly clear what was going to happen.

Fast forward a year. My first therapist had been helpful, but I no longer needed a cheerleader. She had pretty much said, "You're great!" It was just what I needed at the time, but things had changed. The divorce was final, and I now had other problems. Specifically, dating issues.

I consulted a psychiatrist friend of mine, who certainly knew a thing or two about therapists. I tried someone new who came highly recommended; she had a full calendar and charged a hefty fee. She was also downright nasty. I walked out of our sessions feeling so insignificant, so immature, incompetent.... That certainly wasn't a good feeling. She would say things very harshly, like, "Wake up!" as I was baring my soul. I would leave feeling so beaten down...and I was paying for this. I had gone from one extreme to the other. Wasn't there someone who was just right?

I was still convinced of the value of speaking to someone who was not biased, from the outside world—that is, not a personal friend. I leaned on friends frequently, of course, and they were all amazing and supportive, but I still needed something more. I decided to try something different. I reached out to a medium whom I once represented and had the utmost respect for, Alaine Portner...just one more guidepost I tried on the way to finding calm.

Alaine was amazing; she shared messages with me from "beyond." I felt so comforted by the things she shared. She shared messages to me from relatives, which was balm to my broken heart. We talked about signs in my life and how to interpret them. She passed along loving words from my loved ones, including my angel in the sky, my Pop-Pop Al. She was always uplifting; every time I left, I felt great! There is no right or wrong way to seek help; I didn't examine too closely whether this was "real" or not. What mattered was that the comfort I received felt real.

I am not particularly a new-agey sort of person, but around this same time my dear friend from overnight camp, Jami, recommended a book to me. She was upset about the way her career was going; she had recently suffered some setbacks. As we talked she mentioned something about asking the angels for help. I had never heard that before. I said, "What?" "Oh, you don't know about the angels?" she asked. I wasn't quite sure what she meant. I prayed to God of course, but…"Oh, you should pray to the angels too," she said, with great authority.

She recommended that I read *Angels 101* by Doreen Virtue… and, in the spirit of keeping an open mind, I read it. Doreen, a former psychotherapist, is well-known in the new age world as the "angel lady." I found much of value in what she says. I now keep *Angels 101* on my nightstand and am in constant search of signs…and feathers!

Eventually, a friend recommended another therapist, who turned out to be that perfect match. These days, I don't really go to him that much, every month or so, just to check in. Meanwhile, I love the idea of getting guidance from relatives from beyond; it's truly comforting.

Thank you, angels!

CHAPTER 14

Julian was still a baby when I began to notice something strange. It started as a minor annoyance. Jason and I liked to watch TV late at night in our bedroom before falling asleep. Lately, when I laid down and faced the TV on the wall as usual, I could no longer hear if the side of my head was resting on a pillow. I needed to lift my head, and use both ears, to be able to make out what the people on screen were saying. I didn't make too much of this. I was frantically busy, constantly tired, and, besides, what was there to worry about? I had never had a hint of hearing trouble before in my life. I aced every hearing test all through school. Mainly, I was still young. Why on earth would I be worried about my hearing?

But then I started noticing the same problem at work. MB and Associates' downtown office had an open floor plan, with the space divided by movable panels, not full walls. This setup made it easy for us all to simply raise our voices and call out to each other without having to get up, leave our desk, and walk over to the other person's space. I realized I was now having to get up out of my chair and go stand in front of whoever was speaking, because after I heard my name called, I could no longer make out the words. The separate sounds all blended into one steady hum I could not quite hear. This was worrisome. Still, this too I shook off for months.

At a certain point I could no longer ignore how much I was handicapped at work. At this point it was no longer just from far away; I was misunderstanding words that people said directly to my face in regular conversation. My team frequently thought I was joking when in actuality I hadn't heard them correctly. "I'm not trying to be funny. I'm going deaf!" I said after the latest confusing word scramble. Now that really was me trying to make a joke. Who goes deaf before forty?

A couple of months later I woke up feeling like I had water in my ears, as if something hadn't drained properly. Finally admitting defeat, I went to my regular doctor to get checked out. He looked into my ears and said everything looked okay to him. "You might have fluid in your ears, and we may have to put tubes in to drain them." Now that procedure I was familiar with; my daughter had had it done. "Tubes? Adults get tubes?" So, I would be the thirty-eight-year-old with tubes? I couldn't believe it. Perhaps Arielle and I could get a two-for-one discount! The doctor added, I should consult an ear, nose, and throat specialist. I made the appointment.

I took a standard hearing test at the specialist's office to establish a baseline, first thing. It seemed to me that it went fine. I thought I did well. After my test I was ushered into an exam room to wait for the doctor. When he walked in, he was holding a box of tissues. That was surprising. He sat down, introduced himself, and said without hesitation, "I have good news and bad news. Which do you want first?"

"Ummm, the good news I guess."

"The good news is your ears are clear, and you don't need tubes." He paused and held out the box of tissues. "The bad news is that you have significant hearing loss, and I am recommending you get hearing aids." I immediately burst into tears, which he had obviously known I would. He must have assumed, given my age, the diagnosis would not go over well.

The specialist was trying to talk to me about possible causes and next steps, but I could barely comprehend a word he was saying. In spite of the many warning signs, I was stunned. Now I really couldn't hear; it was like a movie, where I could see his lips moving but didn't hear a sound. I left the office in a daze and called Jason immediately. "Jason, I just left the doctor, and I have significant hearing loss, and they want me to get hearing aids! That's how bad it is!" Coincidentally, we had just been through this. Jason's mother had just gotten fitted for hearing aids, but she was a seventy-something-year-old woman. That was appropriate; this was not.

"No way, are you serious? What?" He couldn't believe it; none of us could. Once my mom, dad, and physician brother-in-law got involved, they booked me an appointment with the top ENT in the area, a specialist in Philadelphia. After a great deal of testing, we still didn't have any definitive answers. This sudden, severe hearing loss was so unexplained that my new doctor recommended every test under the sun, including a CAT scan for a possible tumor pressing against my ears. "We're really covering every base," he reassured me...but every test came out clean.

We went over my medical history with a fine-tooth comb. Because I had been on various hormones during my bout with infertility, they might possibly have affected my hearing. Not that the hormones had actually caused hearing loss, but they might have accelerated a weakness in my genetic makeup, creating hearing issues that would not normally surface until much later in life. That seemed unlikely. Still, hearing loss didn't run in my family; I hadn't had a virus or fever; severe hearing loss in someone so relatively young was quite rare. My condition was somewhat of a medical mystery. Still, when it was all said and done it didn't really matter why, but what next.

So, there I was, with two kids under the age of five, being fitted with state-of-the-art hearing aids. The only good news about this was how advanced these devices were. Nothing like the big, bulky hearing aids on older people I remembered from when I was a kid. I also got industrial-strength earplugs; the kind professional musicians wear, to safeguard whatever was left of my precious hearing. I bitterly regretted all my carelessness in the past: concerts, the IFB (or earpiece) I used to have to wear when on the air in news and cheering, just for starters. A recent high school reunion, for example, had been ridiculously loud. I was sure that event alone had pushed the damage over the edge into "significant."

The hearing aids helped, but then along came tinnitus—ringing in the ears—which was distracting and irritating to the extreme. I had so far been spared that common affliction, but as I was adjusting to life with hearing aids I started to hear ringing in my ears at random times. Eventually, it came to the point where it felt as though there was a sound-soother machine set on high inside my head, buzzing steadily at all times. Like most people who suffer from tinnitus—and there are many—I had to learn to simply adjust. It was enough to drive me mad sometimes, but there was no cure.

At one of my doctors' appointments I found myself seated next to another young woman in the waiting room. I was happy to see another patient my age; usually I was surrounded by seniors in this particular doctor's office. I struck up a conversation; we started to talk and compare notes. I told her about my tinnitus, and she said she didn't have that but suffered from chronic vertigo. "I can't take a spinning class, for example; I'd fall right off the bike. I constantly feel nauseous, on the verge of throwing up. It's a horrible handicap." I was immediately so grateful that it hadn't happened to me. I imagined trying to take care of my kids with that affliction and couldn't. I silently gave thanks and counted my blessings.

* * * *

It became just another part of my morning routine: putting in my hearing aids. I wear them most of the time now, certainly always for work and business functions. I have to marvel at the technological advancements; these tiny little units go all the way inside the ear now and are almost invisible. I can still manage to talk face-to-face with people or on the phone without them, but it's definitely a strain. I would not want to do without these aids; they've made such a difference in my life.

In terms of going forward, I am on a wait-and-watch regimen, but the doctor and I have discussed the possibility of cochlear implants later in life. Hopefully, this won't happen for at least another ten to fifteen years or so if at all. Any further loss of hearing is a scary proposition for someone in my profession.

Like anyone who wrestles with a serious medical issue, I suddenly understood how we all take so many things about our bodies and our health for granted, every day. This was a such a wakeup call for me to be appreciative of all I did have: a strong, healthy heart, a cancer-free body, the energy to do all I needed to...so much! I was still breathing. I still had air in my lungs and could walk and run and play with my kids. In short, I learned a lesson about gratitude.

I remembered when my best friend, Ali, miscarried, which was of course extremely sad and upsetting for her, and for me, feeling for her. When she got pregnant again, which happened right away, she hesitated to tell me. She hadn't wanted to rub it in my face when she knew what a struggle I was facing myself, and she didn't. Sure, I was worried about myself, but that had nothing to do with how I felt about her. "I am going to be here for you," I told her. "I am with you. I support you one hundred percent. I could not be happier for you." I meant every word.

Our invaluable nanny Alicia got married around the time I was starting to show signs of unhappiness at home. Actually, she eloped. She kept the news to herself for more than a month. When I found out I was so surprised...and hurt. I couldn't believe she could keep such news from me, as close as we were. I thought we were family.

"I just couldn't tell you," she said. "You're going through so much stuff right now."

"Yes, but meanwhile life is still going on, and I am delighted for you!" I said.

I was reminded of this once again quite recently, when my cousin Jeremy, with whom I am very close, asked me to accompany him while he looked for an engagement ring for his fiancée. He wanted my opinion, but he knew I was suffering through my latest breakup with a difficult on-and-off boyfriend, hardly in the mood for wedding discussions. "Do you still want to come?" he asked. "Because I understand if you don't feel up to it."

"I am still happy for you!" I told him. "I would not miss this! Come on!" and off we went.

Just because I have a bad headache does not mean that others are not in pain. Nor does my having a bad headache keep others from celebrating their own health and happiness. Be thankful for all we have and be present and rejoice for others. That's something we all need to remember!

Top: Me and Carolyn on the front lawn of our family home, 1982.

Bottom: Me, Carolyn, and my parents at my Mom-Mom and Pop-Pop's 50th wedding anniversary dinner, 1992.

Top, clockwise from top left: My mother, my Great-Grandmother, my Mom-Mom Ruth, and my Pop-Pop Al (who I believe is my guardian angel in heaven), 1981.

Bottom: Me on stage at my first Miss Burlington County Scholarship Pageant competition, 1992.

Top left: Me and Carolyn on the beach in Herzliya, Israel during my spring break from classes, 1995.

Top right: Me and Ali on our way home from the Bahamas, 1999.

Left: Me as a Shawnee Renegade Varsity Football Cheerleader, 1991.

Top, inset: Me at my desk in the KTVE-TV newsroom in Monroe, LA, 2000

Top right: Me and Carolyn at an event I was a spokesperson for while anchoring for WICD-TV in Champaign, IL, 2003.

Bottom: Me on location for a story I was covering for News 12 New Jersey, 2001.

Top: Me and my parents on my wedding day, 2005.

Bottom: Me and Arielle, 2009.

Bottom, inset: Arielle and Sydney, 2008.

Top left: Arielle and Julian, 2013.

Top right: Max, 2018.

Right: Me and Max, 2018.

Top: Me and Jenice at the Disney Run, 2018.

Bottom: Left to Right: Dean Cain's mom, fellow contestant, *Today Show* Producer Tammy Filler, fellow contestant, Sheinelle, and me on *The Today Show*, 2017.

Top: Me and Lauren, 2017.

Right: Me and Kristin, 2018.

Top: Me and Michele, 2018.

Bottom: Me and Julian at my Bat Mitzvah party, 2017.

Top: Me, Arielle, and Julian on our first vacation together post-divorce, 2017.

Bottom: Me at my Bat Mitzvah party, 2017.

CHAPTER 15

That was one version of the story of my hearing loss. Like my marriage, which looked picture-perfect on the outside, there were some unsettling circumstances going on at home. There was a tragic, alternate reality to what really happened during this medical crisis of mine.

One year after the doctor had broken the news while handing me a tissue, I'd been through endless tests. I was struggling with tinnitus and getting used to hearing aids. I was still adjusting to my new reality, which shook me to my core. In terms of career alone, this handicap struck at the heart of all my fears. My whole business was communications. I needed to be able to hear, and to talk; it was my livelihood. My hearing impairment made me vulnerable. So much so that I felt that it was a sign that I was supposed to stay in my marriage. Especially later, I would need a partner. In old age, I was looking at total deafness. Cochlear implants. Maybe even having to learn to talk all over again.... It was a terrifying prospect to face alone and I needed and wanted Jason by my side.

At my annual checkup, the audiologist noted yet more hearing loss. This was the woman who worked with me on fitting my hearing aids. She was very concerned and wanted to speak with my doctor directly. "You need a full workup," she told me. "Something really is wrong."

My doctor agreed. Once again, I got a full workup with blood tests for every last possible thing and an MRI to boot. They weren't ruling anything out. They made an appointment with me to go over the results in a week. A few nights later, I was driving home from a shoot with a client. I hit "answer" on my phone and heard, "Mrs. Lichterman?" my married name. "Yes?" I said briskly. "This is the doctor's office," she said. "Your blood work all came back clean, but there was one issue. You tested positive for syphilis."

"What?!" I said, almost running off the road. My mind raced. *Syphilis?* I hadn't heard that word since middle school health classes. "I am not even sure what it is!"

"It is an STD, sexually transmitted disease. Its symptoms include a skin rash, sores around the vulva or anus, swollen glands, weight loss..."

I had to interrupt this horrible checklist. "I absolutely do *not* have any of those symptoms! Not one, not ever!" I protested.

"This could be dormant in your body, with no exterior symptoms. There's no telling how long you've had it. Don't worry, it's probably just a false positive. That is certainly a possibility," the nurse said, hearing the panic in my voice. "In the meantime, I am going to schedule you for another blood test, just to make sure." By now I had pulled over. My mind immediately raced through every person I had ever slept with, all the way back to the years before I got married. There weren't that many—at all!

Being health conscious, I was always freaked out by the possibility of AIDS, so I had always been extremely careful. My old boyfriend from Louisiana, who had been quite a player, flashed into my mind. I had considered him my boyfriend, but he was not the most faithful kind of guy. He was definitely a "ladies' man."

I mentioned this rather surprising news to Jason that night; he said exactly the same thing I had. "What the hell is that?" he asked. I explained; he didn't seem concerned. "It must be some kind of mistake," he said, and moved on. So did I, returning to my regularly scheduled life, which was frantic as always. Thanksgiving was just around the corner; I was planning a huge feast with both of our families in attendance.

* * * *

A few days later I was at the regular family doctor being treated for a sinus infection. He gave me a prescription for some antibiotics, and I passed the blood lab on my way to fill it. *I should just run inside and get this blood drawn*, I thought. I couldn't take the test while on medication. I quickly ran inside and got my blood drawn again for the confirmation test. I knew this was a testing error that would soon be cleared up.

That night I was chatting on the phone with my best friend, Ali, as we did two or three times a week. She also had two young kids; we used to laugh and commiserate about the sad state of our sex lives with two little ones. Of course, I filled her in on all the latest.

"You don't have syphilis," Ali said. "No way. Unless, of course, Jason is cheating on you," she joked and laughed.

"Are you kidding? He shows no interest in me, and I'm right here under his roof. He wouldn't waste the effort to go out and find someone else. Two women, are you kidding? One is plenty!" That possibility hadn't even crossed my mind, not for a minute. We had problems, of course, but not that kind. "Why would you say that?"

"Well, because they test you for everything, including syphilis, when you're pregnant, so if you contracted it, this had to have happened fairly recently. Since Julian was born," she pointed out. I hadn't even paid attention at that time to the many standard tests; there had been nothing out of the ordinary with my second pregnancy.

"But you don't have it, so don't worry about it," she said reassuringly.

That night Jason was half asleep, with the television playing low in the background. I looked over at him and said very tentatively, "Jason?"

"Yeah?" he mumbled.

"You didn't ever...cheat on me, did you?" I asked.

His head popped up. He looked at me. "What, Mindie?" he asked.

"I know, I know," I said, starting to backtrack immediately. "Ali and I were joking about it tonight.... She was saying that would be the only way it could happen, because I didn't have it...this syphilis thing...when I was pregnant with Julian..."

He shook his head at me reprovingly and went to sleep. This was really crazy. I needed to get hold of myself.

Driving back from the shore that weekend, with the kids in the back of my SUV, I made the familiar eighty-minute drive home on autopilot. As I turned into our neighborhood my Ugg boot got caught under the brake and stuck; I lost control of the vehicle. We slammed into a neighbor's parked car. The crash was so bad, the cars had to be towed away. The neighbors were not pleased. I was going deaf and couldn't even get diagnosed properly. In this week before a major holiday, the rental car agency only had a huge pickup truck available; it wasn't exactly "me." It was black, with huge tires. I had to literally jump up and down to get in and out of the front seat.

Oh, and I was just about to turn forty. Happy birthday to me! I told myself, at least things couldn't get any worse.

* * * *

Thursday night, one week before Thanksgiving, at the end of a long day at the office. I was just putting on my coat, preparing to leave and meet Jason at the house so we could go together to Arielle's kindergarten parent/teacher conference. Our first. I was walking out the door when the phone rang. Same nurse. "Mrs. Lichterman, I'm really sorry to inform you, but your latest test also came back positive for syphilis. You need to be seen by an infectious disease specialist right away." I froze. In that moment, it became stunningly obvious that Jason had indeed done something wrong. That was the only way this could even be a possibility.

I drove home in a daze; Alicia prepared dinner for the kids. The meal was strained. When it was over, Jason and I got into his car to make the short drive to the elementary school. "Jason, the doctor's office called again. I do have syphilis," I said flatly.

"What?"

"Yes. I do. And there's only one way that could have happened."

He denied any wrongdoing, vehemently. He swore he had not cheated on me, ever. I cut him off. "I don't want to do this now. Later. We need to talk tonight, after this conference, because there's something you have to tell me. I need you to tell me what you have done, because this is very serious." He was speechless; he gripped the steering wheel. The rest of the ride was silent.

Our parent/teacher conference was a waste of time; I didn't hear a word Arielle's teacher said. I could not concentrate on her drawings and paintings and the many examples of lettering and numbers I was being shown. I couldn't pay any attention to this important milestone in my child's life at all. I missed the entire meeting. I was there, but in body only as I automatically smiled and nodded. My mind was a million miles away, frantic.

That night, after I'd put the kids to bed, I entered our bedroom. My husband was lying on his back, staring up at the ceiling. "Jason," I said. He looked over at me reluctantly. I looked him full on in the face and said, "Please, just tell me what you did. I need to know. Whatever you did, I will forgive you, but you need to tell me, because this is affecting my health and we have small children. Julian's just a baby. Please!"

At the mention of the kids he broke down. "I did something. When I was in Denver on a trip last year I visited a massage parlor. I paid extra for a blow job. That's all, I swear."

Though I had known it must be true, I couldn't believe my ears. He proceeded to try to explain, but I'd heard all I cared to. The only thing I wanted to do now was find out if this could really happen. I would later see through google searches on medical sites it was indeed possible. So, he wasn't hooking up with another woman. He had visited, basically, a prostitute... which was so much worse. Now I was convinced I had every conceivable disease, up to and including HIV. My mind conjured up every possible dire scenario under the sun.

This possibility, of course, was in addition to my carrying a nasty disease the New Jersey Board of Health thought had been wiped out decades ago, and they said as such when they called me to make sure I was seeking treatment. My mind raced about how I'd been carrying this for a year, never suspecting a thing. I felt disgusting, dirty, betrayed, foolish. My kitchen downstairs was overflowing with groceries and supplies for our Thanksgiving dinner. I could not think of a single thing to be thankful about.

CHAPTER 16

Needless to say, Jason slept in the guest room that night. I didn't close my eyes; I gazed unseeingly into the dark, thinking even darker thoughts. All I wanted to do was to get help. To be fixed! I was on the phone bright and early the next morning, asking the doctor if, in the course of all those blood tests, he'd tested me for HIV. He hadn't. There had been no reason to.

The timing could not have been worse with the holidays approaching. There was no way I could manage to book an appointment with an infectious disease specialist in the few short days remaining before Thanksgiving. I couldn't work and I was a complete basket case. Jason, meanwhile, headed off to his own doctor for his own blood test.

I spent the afternoon on the phone with my original doctor's office. I told the nurse the whole story. "Please, what is the treatment?" I asked. I wanted it out of me, now!

"It depends on what stage you are in. It's likely this is now neurosyphilis, so it's quite invasive," she said. "I'm not going to lie to you. It's an IV treatment, similar to chemotherapy. It will take a month, and you'll be in and out of the hospital to get this completely out of your system. We'll start with a spinal tap first, to see how advanced it is." I could not believe what I was hearing.

For the next five days, I thought I was going to die. Literally. I was sure I had HIV. We had just seen the movie *Dallas Buyer's Club* the week before; the image of Matthew McConaughey's gaunt, AIDS-ridden body would not leave my mind. My brother-in-law, a doctor, called in a favor to get me in to see an infectious disease specialist the next Monday afternoon. The weekend was torture. I vacillated between rage and stopping myself from throwing Jason out, to thinking I would soon be bedridden and need help with the children. I didn't know what to do. Julian was still in diapers!

On Saturday I could barely function; I sent the kids off to my in-laws. I sat on the sofa in the finished basement googling "massage parlors, Denver" and perusing articles about why husbands cheat. I was getting quite an education. Reading myself into a frenzy. I learned more than I ever wanted to know about that particular kind of business in Denver, complete with graphic reviews on Yelp.

"So, I have a question," I said, after I marched upstairs and into the guest room.

Jason looked at me warily. "What?" I launched into a grilling he could not believe. I demanded to know exactly what he did, with whom, where, which place.... I was possessed. I would not stop. I wanted every last detail. I was flipping out!

He couldn't take it. "You want to know what I did?"

"Of course, I want to know what you did! What, is the story going to change now? That's another lie, the massage parlor?"

Turned out yes, it was. He'd been in the hotel bar in Denver, met a girl, hooked up with her. It was just a blow job, he swore, with a one-night stand. Here was a real good news/bad news scenario. She wasn't a professional sex worker in a seedy massage parlor, so she was less likely to have something like HIV, but the implications were far more disturbing. My husband had had an actual one-night stand. Then, for an entire year, he had looked me in the eye and never thought he should confess to me? Had the shoe been on the other foot, the guilt would have eaten me alive. The fact that he had kept it a secret was almost worse than the betrayal.

* * * *

I sat in the sanctuary of the temple after dropping Julian off at his preschool class that Monday morning. My hearing issue, so paramount just a week before, had receded far into the background. Now I just wanted to live. "Please God, do not let me die. Just don't let me have HIV. Let me be all right for my kids, and I will take it as a sign to leave this marriage."

"Mom, if I'm HIV positive, just take me to Ancora and drop me off, because I cannot handle it!" I told my mother in one of my more hysterical outbursts on the way to the infectious disease specialist that afternoon. Ancora is the New Jersey insane asylum. I did not think I was strong enough to endure that particular scenario. "Just tell them to put me to sleep!" Clearly, I was losing my mind. I couldn't believe how fast my life had turned upside down.

* * * *

The highly regarded infectious disease doctor was very cold, no bedside manner at all. He listened expressionlessly as I explained, in front of my parents, what my husband had told me and how I could have been exposed to an STD. It was beyond mortifying. He did a quick preliminary external exam and took my history yet again. "When can I get started on the treatment?" I asked.

"I'm not going to start you on anything just yet. I am not convinced you have syphilis," he said. "I am going to run my own blood work. When I get it back, and if it's positive, we'll start you on a treatment plan." He gave me the scrip to go to the lab and get blood drawn yet again. My mother and I raced over there like I was on fire. I could not wait to get going with this.

"Mom, what if I don't have anything wrong with me?" I said. "How crazy would that be?"

"Mindie." My mom was trying to be reasonable with me. Support me but prepare me for my reality. "You've had a number of tests that say..."

"I know, I know, I'm just saying." Then Jason called me.

"I got my lab work back, and it's negative. I don't have syphilis." He let that sink in for a moment. "Do you have something you want to tell me?"

"Actually, yes, I do have something to tell you. Then I don't have it either. This doctor wasn't sure I did to begin with. How about that?" I could not believe that he would try to turn this on me!

The next day the infectious disease doctor called me. My blood work was back. I didn't have syphilis, or any other sort of STD. After two false positives, this was definitive. He swore to it; he would stake his reputation on it. It was quite a difficult Thanksgiving. Jason and I celebrated the day separately; he with his parents, the kids and I with mine. I had some serious thinking to do.

Cue the predictable decision to get counseling. Jason finally agreed to go, something I had been begging him to do forever. He had always refused. At this point he finally agreed; he was remorseful; he was sweet and loving; he showered me with presents. Which I didn't really want. I had only ever wanted his attention. Any solo trips on his part were over, that was for sure. Had he been engaged in an actual ongoing affair, with romantic feelings involved, I would have left in a heartbeat. I decided to stay and try to work things out. If we could. I realized our relationship would never be the same.

Also, predictably, six months later, he had slipped back into his old ways—we both had—and I had adjusted to both my hearing loss and my new reality. I had come to look at this as a blessing. I would never have dreamed of leaving my marriage until my kids were both grown, if I had believed that my husband was faithful. I was sure he was; that was one thing I didn't worry about. I had been dead set on making things work until those kids were raised and in college. They deserved a happy, stable, "normal" home and I was hell-bent on providing it to them. My own happiness could wait.

Still, two false positives? This was such a sign. One mistake could easily happen, but two? I had to believe this was a push from the universe. It was trying to tell me something.

Power Passage #6

LOVE YOUR PET

"Dogs come into our lives to teach us about love; they depart to teach us about loss. A new dog never replaces an old dog. It merely expands the heart."

—AUTHOR UNKNOWN

Sydney, all eleven pounds of him, was the very heart of my heart: a fluffy white Maltese I acquired in the aftermath of a broken engagement, while still in my twenties. I had accepted a news job in a small town far from home where I knew absolutely no one, and I wanted a companion. He proved to be my absolute truest companion for the next sixteen years. He also taught me how to care for another creature, to be responsible, to worry about another life. As I moved all over the map seemingly every year for nearly a decade, my dog meant "home" to me. No matter what crazy hours I worked, no matter what time I raced out the door in a mad rush to cover a story, he was always there to greet me in whatever little apartment I was living in at the time.

In 2015, things were not going well at our house. Unhappy and unfulfilled in my marriage, I was trying to work up the courage to leave when I was hit with a double blow. My mom was diagnosed with breast cancer for the second time—twelve years after the first bout, in what the doctors said was a completely unrelated reoccurrence—and Sydney was fading fast. He was terribly sick, terminally so. The day came when we had run out of options. It was time; I had to put him down. Jason wanted to come with me to the vet, but I said no. I appreciated the fact that my husband loved this dog too; he had lived with him for ten years, after all. Still, I was with Sydney first, and it had started out as just the two of us. I wanted it to be that way at the end. So, it was. I held him and spoke to him gently as he closed his eyes for the last time. He exited this earth in the arms of the person who loved him best in the world.

Syd was my life, but even I would concede that he was not the best behaved or most well-trained dog. In fact, to be honest, he was a bad dog. He was pretty much a one-woman pet. Around any other people, he barked, he snapped. I couldn't take him anywhere because he attacked everything—people and objects alike. Whenever well-meaning friends or strangers approached to see the cute dog, I had to ward them off. "Don't touch, don't touch, he's not friendly!" This was my mantra for years and years. None of this affected my love for him at all, but it was trying. He also never really took to housebreaking, was a finicky eater, and was not particularly great around kids, even my own. Syd was the worst. And the best...like I said. He was everything.

With Syd gone, I fell into a deep state of mourning. Any thoughts of unhappiness in my marriage receded; I could not handle another loss after Sydney. He had been mine in a very special way. Yes, I had a husband and children, but he took me all the way back, a reminder of earlier, carefree days, just the two of us against the world. Looking into his eyes gave me a special kind of comfort no one and nothing else could. When he died, I wanted to die too. "I want to be on the Rainbow Bridge with him," I cried one night as my mom tried in vain to comfort me. "I don't want to be here. I just want to be with Syd!"

"Mindie, you have children," my mom reminded me sternly. I didn't mean it, of course. I eventually pulled it together for my kids, but that's how bad I felt. I pestered Jason to design a special commemorative bracelet for me, engraved with an S for Sydney, and wore it all the time. He was more than a little worried about me. I boxed up Sydney's stuff and put it away, out of sight. It hurt too much to see his things.

Six weeks or so after Sydney passed away, I was scanning the Petfinder ads. It was much too soon to think about another dog, of course, but I wanted to explore adoption for the future. Sydney had been a dog with papers and a pedigree from a breeder. I had become much more aware in the years since then. I wanted to rescue the next dog, whenever he was meant to come. For now, I just wanted some more information on how the process worked. And then I saw that face. An adorable puppy. "Jason, look at this baby," I called over to him. "What do you think?"

"Cute," said Jason. "Want to go look at him?"

"No, it's much too soon," I said, and put the iPad away. But the next night, I looked again. There was that face again. The next night, same thing. I could not stop looking at this perfect little face. I picked up the phone and asked the volunteer on the other end about this puppy.

"We're showing him this weekend at our PetSmart adoption fair if you'd like to come out."

Immediate panic set in. "Oh my God, someone is going to snatch him up immediately if you take him out to a fair! Can I please see him before then?"

"Well, you can come tonight, if you like, but if you want him, you will have to take him. We don't reserve dogs. If you don't take him with you, we will take him to the fair this weekend."

Jason and I packed up the kids and went off to see this puppy at his foster home. There were some absolutely adorable puppies there, but I was drawn like a magnet to Max, a shih tzu with the happiest, most playful temperament. Watching him run and tumble eased my heart for the first time in weeks. I fell in love with Max on the spot, and sure enough, we wound up taking him home. We had to stop on the way home to buy all new supplies. It was a new beginning.

Here's the thing. Max is my new love. He is my city dog. I dress him up and we walk the New York streets together. He comes with me to the salon. I take him to work. He is mellow and friendly and greets everyone with a wagging tail. He loves both my kids, and they love him right back. He's a great traveler. I can smuggle him onto the bus to New York in his carrier because he never makes a peep.

I truly believe that God rewarded me with an easygoing dog, because Max is an angel. Love is so sweet the second time around!

CHAPTER 17

No matter how badly it ended—and I suffered through some pretty bad moments indeed in the intermission after my divorce—I will always be grateful for the good. My friend and work colleague Shane brought a big part of me back from the dead, and for that I will be eternally grateful! I believe he was my soulmate, for many different reasons, though I also believe we are all quite capable of more than one soulmate in life, if we are lucky and have open hearts. I met him as a business contact; he quickly became my confidante. And he eventually gave me the final push I needed to leave my marriage.

The initial attraction was purely professional. After my first client appeared in his magazine, we worked together frequently. Shane was so sharp, so bright. Super smart and well-read, in addition to being Jewish, with a news background, both big plusses for me. He came from a nice solid family. In fact, through his stories and our shared day-to-day talks on the phone, by text, and in person, his family reminded me very much of my own. We shared a common background with similar upbringings.

I came to admire so many things about him, both personally and professionally. In terms of work, he was an ideal sounding board. He brainstormed with me. He offered good advice and a new perspective about some of my business and personnel issues. Mainly, he was unfailingly supportive. He told me many times that I should open a New York City office for MB and Associates. In short, he encouraged me to dream big. I had lost sight of my dreams, lately. He brought many of them back.

As we grew closer and I began to confide in him about my marriage, I learned more about Shane's own troubles too. He and his on-and-off again girlfriend, Anne, who lived in Wilmington, Delaware, seemed to have a dysfunctional exis-tence. Shane often shared how incompatible they were. Anne would sometimes come to stay on the weekends at his home in Gladwyne. They had recently broken up—again—after she complained bitterly about the size of a ring he had given her for a recent birthday present. They fought constantly and he complained about things to me quite often. I could never under-stand why he stayed with her.

One day, over coffee, Shane told me that Anne had said to him, more than once, "You know, I think you're secretly in love with Mindie." *What an insecure, paranoid woman*, is what I thought at that moment. I was honestly surprised. I was still married, and those vows—and my kids' security and happi-ness—were things I took seriously. However, my marriage was crumbling, fast. Gradually our friendship began edging toward something more when Shane became quite flirty. Never crossing the line, but just a bit more than "friendly." We talked daily and texted all the time. But it was harmless.

One of my clients was being featured in his magazine, and we both wound up at the photo shoot. The sexual tension was palpable; something was most definitely in the air. "Love ya," he texted as I was driving home, giving me a jolt. I wondered what was going on with us. He called soon afterward, but I was on the phone with a reporter and couldn't get off. When I returned the call, he must have lost his nerve, because things were strictly back to business and the upcoming holiday issue of his publication. We discussed my upcoming business trip to Chicago and hung up. Still, the door had been kicked open. I really liked him; I felt something more than I should for him. I had to get out of my marriage, because we were not the kind to cheat. I needed to end it.

I had numerous issues on my trip to Chicago. Everything went wrong, from flights being canceled to car rental mix-ups. Normally, I would call my office or my dad, if I had encountered an issue on the road, but it was after hours for the office and my dad was out of pocket. So, when Shane emailed to check on me at 3,500 feet, I asked him for help, and he quickly straightened everything out. The next morning, he called me, on his way to work. It was super early in Chicago, and the phone scared me out of a sound sleep.

"Hey, I just wanted to see if you were okay," he said.

"I'm fine, thanks for calling," I mumbled, barely awake.

"Great, go back to sleep," he said, and hung up. But one minute later my phone beeped. "Now I know what you sound like in the morning. And you me. You sound hot." It had been ages since I'd engaged in this kind of banter. I had been frozen for so long. Sure, I had known I wasn't happy, but I could barely recall the last time I'd felt the opposite. It had been years since I'd felt excited, buzzed, fluttery over possibilities. I had thought such feelings might be gone forever. We flirted madly back and forth the rest of the day. While waiting to board my flight home, I texted Shane: "You're brave on text but not in person. Can we talk?"

"You know I have feelings for you. But you're married. I'm in a relationship. It's complicated."

"You're not happy and neither am I," I countered. "We should be together!"

"This is not a conversation to text. Let's meet in person." We set a dinner meeting a couple weeks ahead, because we were both that busy. In a quiet restaurant, on the Main Line, near Shane's home, we talked about everything. Our feelings, our relationships, our future...was there one? Not at the moment, but we decided that we would both respectfully end our relationships and reconvene to see what might be possible. Soon afterward, I respectfully ended mine by actually asking for a divorce. Shane respectfully did not end his. So that was that!

* * * *

Spring of 2016, after my heart-to-heart with Jason. The one that had taken all my courage. The one where we established that, yes, we were going to go ahead and divorce. I was headed into New York for a client meeting, in a very grumpy mood. Life was so uncertain; I was not feeling particularly cheery about anything. Our suburban New Jersey train station is a good hour and a half out of the city, though plenty of people make the commute daily. There are numerous stops along the way, picking up and dropping off commuters. It was late afternoon when a young man boarded. There were several empty seats, but he plopped down next to me. I glanced at him briefly and registered a nice-looking guy—really young, twenties. I returned to my newspaper.

But he wanted to talk. Ugh! He started asking me about my horoscope and making jokes. Marc was handsome, but he was just *so young*. I couldn't quite figure out what he wanted. Why all the chatter? He was asking me where I was going, and what I did for a living. He wouldn't shut up! Though I was irritated, I politely answered. Until he asked me out. I looked at him in real surprise. "Trust me. You don't want to date me."

"Why not?"

"I am significantly older than you.... How old *are* you, by the way?"

"Twenty-six," he replied.

"Twenty-six! Your mother would kill you! Listen. I have kids, two of them. I am the last thing you want."

"You're the ultimate MILF!" he gasped.

"I know you mean that in a good way, but it's not exactly a compliment," I said and laughed. He professed not to believe that I was forty-two. He wasn't deterred on hearing my age, at all. He continued to talk the entire way into the city, telling me about his financial job—he was a hedge fund trader, from a good family. A really appealing young man altogether. But the whole idea was ridiculous; I couldn't take him seriously. When we got off, I handed him my business card, mainly because he was so relentless about obtaining it. I exited the train and headed to my meeting.

The next week, after a client meeting in Philadelphia, I met Shane for lunch. We really had things out. I poured out my heart. It was very heavy and emotional as I confessed my feelings...again, which he swore he reciprocated. "Then I don't understand why you don't leave her. You've said it's been over for months!" I finished.

"I can't break up with her now. She is on the verge of a nervous breakdown; she hates her job, she hates her life; I just can't abandon her," he told me. It was agonizing to hear this. In my gut, right at that moment I knew it was time for a major reset. I should gather myself. Pull back. Guard my heart. Just then my phone beeped. The guy from the train, Marc, was texting. "I think you are so beautiful. When are you going to be back in New York again, let's have dinner." I shook my head but had to smile.

"Who's that?" Shane asked instantly. Jealously. Which was absolutely ridiculous, considering the speech he had just given me. He had no right.

"Some guy I met on the train last week. It's nothing," I said. I had no intention of ever seeing Marc again. Really, I should have resolved to never see Shane again. But the next day my great friend and admirer, the one who checked in on me constantly, hung on every word that came out of my mouth, treated me like a princess, backed me up on everything, considered nothing too much trouble if it made me happy...that guy was back. The warmth and friendship he offered was too hard to resist. I couldn't stay away.

CHAPTER 18

Back when we were at that difficult point when Jason and I were still living in the same house, the lawyer I had hired to file for divorce for me had cautioned me at one point. He said, "You absolutely should not date at this juncture. Keep things peaceful; don't give him any reason to get vindictive or nasty." Reluctantly, I agreed. Jason and I were barely speaking. He was demanding all the jewelry he had ever given me back, which meant every present I'd ever received in my marriage. I had no privacy because he was just down the hall. Shane remained elusive. I was completely miserable. I was complaining to my friend Lori about Shane on the phone one day. "He still won't leave her. I don't understand...."

"You're in no position to call anyone out about anything, Mindie," she said.

"What do you mean? I'm officially separated! We'll be divorced any minute!"

"Oh, come on, you're still living in the same house with Jason! Who's to say you won't go back with him? This guy doesn't know if you're really ever splitting. Look, forget about what Shane's doing. You need to focus on yourself and your kids. Have a little fun on the side with him if you want, but that's it. For now, anyway."

She was right, but this was a very cold-blooded approach and something I just couldn't do. Shane likely couldn't either. So, we decided to stay friends and not to cross a line. If it was meant to be later—it would. So, instead, I fully shifted focus solely onto my kids, my business, and my reinvention as a soon-to-be newly minted single woman.

Still, I had to examine just what was it about this man that had captivated me so completely. Deep down inside Shane was a great person. I saw the warm and wonderful heart underneath all his present issues. But honestly...did it matter why? We had crazy chemistry! After the long dry spell that had been my marriage, this kind of excitement was so intoxicating. He had told me frequently how beautiful I was. How interesting. Once again, I had felt desirable. Just by his words, he warmed up a part of me that had all but withered away from neglect. "I'm going to be your prince one day," he would say to me. But for now, I was not going to be a damsel in distress. Just like in Israel, I was counting on me. Mindie.

I had learned so much in my marriage: about living together, compromising, raising children with another person. I learned plenty about myself during our divorce as well, including the major realization that a passionless marriage was not going to work for me. Any future possible relationship with Shane—or anyone!—would have to include not just an emotional connection but a physical one too. Passion and excitement and desire would become part of my life again. And I was going to go all in, throwing caution to the wind, completely abandoning any thought of being protective of my own heart. I would dive in deep! I had a lot to look forward to.

* * * *

The dating scene was certainly different this time around. I quickly came to realize that online was simply the accepted way many people met now, even though it still seemed unnatural to me. So, I gave it a try. I joined a dating app called J-Swipe and began talking with a couple of different guys. They were Jewish, obviously; my faith had become much more important to me than it used to be. Not that being Jewish guaranteed anything....

Dating was all about texting these days, which certainly brought out a lot of false courage in men. I received a number of texts where all I could think was, *Ummmm, I wasn't ready to see that.* Yes, things had certainly changed in the single decade I'd been out of the dating pool. It was a whole new world out there because of social media and online dating.

A plastic surgeon, super good looking. He and I were going to meet for a drink; we just had to arrange our schedules. My phone was lying on the kitchen counter early one morning. I was making the kids' lunches. I heard the phone buzz and picked it up. There was a close-up of his bare ass. "Want to see a *really* sexy one?" he asked.

"No thanks!" I replied immediately. What the hell? I could not understand the sexting going on all the time from these random dates I hadn't even met yet! Gross!

Then there were the setups, from a plethora of friends and acquaintances with good intentions. One guy in particular sounded ideal. He was witty and fun in his initial conversations with me. A Jewish doctor from New York with a psychotherapy practice—perfect! We were chatting back and forth, flirting just a bit, and making plans to get together and meet. He emailed me, "When are you in the city again? Where could we meet? Here's what I'm thinking. We could have a drink...and if there's chemistry, have another drink, and go back to your place...repeat."

I wrote back, somewhat frostily, "We could have a drink and, a bit later on after a few more dates, we can see what unfolds." I saw that he read the message but didn't reply, and never contacted me again. That was the end of that. So, that's what was out there.... This from a doctor, no less. He was no doubt counseling people, presumably quite a few women, on love and relationships, when all he was looking to do was get in bed on the first date. Sigh. I was surprised that so many men assumed, maybe because I was older, that I was going to sleep with them as soon as I met them. Not the case! No thanks!

The guy from the train stayed in touch. Marc was persistent, I had to give him that. He texted every now and then, sporadically, in the months ahead. Every once in a while my phone would buzz with a last-minute invitation, something like, "Hey, want to go to the Knicks game tonight?" It always made me laugh, because it was so obvious how young he was, still doing stuff on the spur of the moment. I was an overscheduled, overstressed single mom; I couldn't drop work or my kids' events to join him.

"I'll take your kids on my boat," he offered one day. *OMG, my kids aren't meeting you*, was all I could think. Marc receded into background noise, because dating a millennial was one thing I did not see happening. My heart wasn't really in the dating scene, anyway. Sadly, my heart still longed for Shane. But I kept pushing forward. I had to move on. I concentrated on more spiritual pursuits, healing myself, the bigger picture.

Power Passage #7

THE WORLD WON'T COME TO YOUR DOOR... GET OUT THERE

"Opportunities multiply as they are seized."

—SUN TZU

My friend, journalist Jenice Armstrong, and I worked on a special, ongoing project together for more than a decade. The *Philadelphia Daily News's* Sexy Singles was an annual summer four-day feature put on by the *Philadelphia Daily News* and Philly.com. We accepted nominations for "sexy singles" from the entire Greater Philadelphia region and nominated our own VIPs each year, which included professional sports figures, news talent, and local celebrities. We judged the entrants on a variety of criteria, because there are so many elements that contribute to what makes someone "sexy." Age was not a factor; we wanted to mix it up between men and women, twenties, forties, and sixties, a bus driver, a single dad, a firefighter, a grandmother.

Davy Jones, the original Monkee, who had retired to a horse farm in Pennsylvania, was a very popular "sexy single"!

My office would contact the chosen singles and schedule their photo shoot, which took place over three days in early June. It was all quite glamorous—well, not for Davy Jones maybe, but for most regular folks it was quite a treat to be made over professionally from head to toe, from makeup to hair to a new outfit, styled by me and a stylist I worked with, Anthony Henderson. We pulled swimsuits, clothes, and accessories from a variety of high-end boutiques and local designers throughout the area. The "models" were then shot by the esteemed *Daily News* photojournalists on location, usually in Atlantic City: by the pool at Caesars, for example, or on the boardwalk. We worked from sunrise to sunset for three consecutive days styling and photographing the singles for their profiles.

We usually had a pool of thirty or so winners, because invariably some of the singles were not quite as marketable as we had thought, let's say, and had to be removed after we spent an hour with them talking and shooting. A couple got cold feet. Once the spread hit the stands, I would then book Jenice for an abundance of press appearances. She would appear on the radio and on TV to promote the spread; sometimes I might join her on the air. The print and online feature usually ran in mid-August, every day from Monday through Thursday. The finale was a lavish gala complete with a red carpet and a VIP reception. The event was then open to the public to meet and mingle with that summer's group of Who's Who. We held the event at various trendy locations around Philly: the Stratus Lounge rooftop at the Hotel Monaco; the Water Works in Fairmount Park; Parx Casino in Pennsylvania.... Every year it was the party of the year, a very high-profile event!

During the last two years I worked on this project, I myself had suddenly become a "single." Plenty of people asked, "Why aren't you a 'sexy single,' Mindie?" As a judge and someone who helped to spearhead the project, I wasn't allowed. I couldn't even nominate my own clients, some of whom would have been perfect. It would have been a conflict of interest. Not to mention, it was a little too soon to be out celebrating singlehood, quite honestly; the first year I wasn't exactly feeling "sexy" or "single." Still, it was a really fun event, something I would have loved to participate in.

Jump ahead to a hot summer day a year later. As I was driving to work one morning I hit a curb with my car and blew out a tire. I was just sitting on the side of the road, waiting for someone to come rescue me, when I got a call from Manhattan. I didn't recognize the number, but I picked it up because I thought with a 212-area code it was probably a news outlet. Sure enough, it was my dear friend Sheinelle Jones, a very talented anchor on *The Today Show*. She and I met when she was a local anchor at Fox in Philadelphia, and just like Lauren, we became fast friends. I fell in love with her genuine spirit and kind heart. I'm so proud of all she's accomplished and incredibly thankful for the friendship she and I share! She's hard to track down sometimes as she's unbelievably busy, so I was excited to hear her voice on the other end.

Dean Cain, aka Superman, was guest-hosting the show during the nine a.m. hour, alongside Sheinelle, before they started the changeover to *Megyn Kelly Today*. As they bantered back and forth about his love life, it was revealed on-air that Mr. Cain, somehow, was currently very single. Producers thought it would be fun to do a spoof of *The Dating Game* on the show. They were looking for bachelorettes, and Sheinelle was calling to say she had nominated me. I was thrilled! She had chosen me, a producer had picked one contestant, and Dean's mother chose a woman from L.A.

Now I didn't really think I might end up in a relationship with Dean Cain, though that would be quite pleasant. Really, I looked at this opportunity as a real coup for MB and Associates, and a very flattering vote of confidence from my friend, who thought of me out of her many talented and beautiful single friends. Also, I am never one to turn down a chance to go on camera! Of course, I brought the girls from my office along with me on show day. We all rode together in a black town car to *The Today Show* studio in Rockefeller Center. The show's hair stylist and makeup artist glammed me up, and then we did a fun little spoof to stretch over two segments on live, national TV.

As the familiar game show music played, Dean was hidden by a barrier as he asked us all various questions. We three ladies sat on stools to the side, trying to intrigue him with our answers. I was Bachelorette Number Three. "What would you like to say to Dean, Bachelorette Number Three?" they asked for my first question. "Hello, Dean," I said. "I often go by Wonder Woman. I think I am one, at least in my own mind." He thought that was funny; it went on from there.

In the end, I was passed up. I did not get chosen by Dean; he went with his mom's choice. I think there may have been some secret signaling going on, because he did make a nice remark about me the next day on the air. I tweeted him saying, "Thanks for the shout-out!" and he tweeted me back. It was all very unexpected and fun. When opportunities for events like these come along, grab them! You never know where they will lead, or when the next opportunity will knock!

CHAPTER 19

When I had become a mom, I committed to my children having a Jewish upbringing. Though I'd skipped a bat mitzvah myself, it was certainly something I wanted for my kids. Once my daughter began preparations for her own coming-of-age ceremony, to be held when she turned thirteen, I got paid back for every bit of whining I had done as a child. Granted, it was a lot.

Arielle attended a Jewish preschool and then started going to religious school in kindergarten, studying the meaning of the holidays and the cultural aspects of Judaism. In first grade, she began Hebrew school in addition to Sunday school, on Wednesday nights. It's an hour and a half in the synagogue to learn the language, prayers, and so forth. So, lessons in the middle of the week on top of regular school and Sunday school...like mother, like daughter. Arielle complained to me. Frequently. "Mommy...you weren't bat mitzvahed, why do I have to do it?" was the most frequent question.

"Because I made a mistake. I should not have skipped it, and you are learning from my mistake. That's why," was my answer.

I wanted to set a good example—for both my kids. I also wanted to truly understand the prayers and rituals at temple, instead of just showing up for high holy days, when I would sit in shul and not really be able to follow the intricacies of the ceremonies. I had no idea what and why were we saying what we did. I vaguely recognized the chants throughout the service, but only because I had heard them so often. I didn't even really understand the basic significance of the *aliyah*—being called to the *bimah* (stage) to recite a blessing over the Torah.

When it came time for me to stand on the bimah with Arielle and even Julian down the line, I wanted to know what I was doing. I wanted to actually understand why I was doing it. I wanted to look like a Jewish person, because I am. A proud one!

* * * *

Just as Jason and I had finished our divorce proceedings, a male Jewish friend of mine asked me if I was going to get a *get*. A *get* is a Jewish divorce decree, one that I needed to have should I ever want to remarry in the synagogue. It's basically the Jewish equivalent to an annulment in the Catholic church. In the interests of planning ahead and getting all my ducks in a row, I investigated it. I learned that the *get* is an official document, presented in front of witnesses in a small ceremony, and that without it, whatever we did according to civil law was meaningless. Without a *get*, Jason and I would remain officially married, forever—at least in the eyes of Jewish law.

In the Jewish faith, the soon-to-be ex-husband officially grants the wife the *get*, though both parties must agree to the divorce. Jason, fortunately, was agreeable, so we began the process. It actually took much longer to get the *get* than it did for our legal divorce. There was a great deal of paperwork in terms of getting sign-offs and various documents filed. I hadn't realized a *get* was an actual mini ceremony. On the appointed day, we gathered in the synagogue office: me, the senior rabbi, the younger rabbi, and three witnesses. I burst into tears; the solemn ritual was much more than I was emotionally prepared for. I knew that I was moving into my own house in the next couple of weeks, and it struck me how truly over this marriage really was. Not for the first time, of course, but in a very deep and irrevocable way.

The younger rabbi asked me to come into his office to talk at the conclusion of the *get* ceremony. He didn't see that much of me. I showed up at the synagogue for high holidays, and I dropped my daughter off every week for her Hebrew school classes, but he didn't know me well at all. Mainly what he knew was that I was a well-known publicist in the area who had gotten divorced. Obviously. We chatted for a bit about Arielle, and he asked me if I had been bat mitzvahed myself. "No, but it's something I would like to do," I told him.

"Funny you should say that. We are just about to start our adult b'nai mitzvah class." This was official preparation for a bar or bat mitzvah, with multiple people receiving instruction at the same time in a classroom setting.

"Oh no, this is not the time," I told the rabbi. "As you know, I just got divorced. We're moving in the next couple of weeks. I'm frantically busy at work. I just can't do it right now."

"We only offer this class every five years, so the time really is now. I highly encourage you to think about it."

I wasn't feeling super confident about being able to pull off any more than I already had in my overscheduled, newly single-mom life. The timing was not great, but.... "Let me give it some thought," I said.

I briefly flashed back to my trip to Israel and my boyfriend, Ayal the hairdresser. I remembered that I had been afraid to tell him that I hadn't been bat mitzvahed; it seemed especially wrong in Israel somehow. I was a little worried about what he would think. I shouldn't have been. Ayal had laughed. "Mindie, that's such an American thing," he'd said. In Israel, men and women were strictly separated during orthodox services. Very few Israeli girls were bat mitzvahed. Americans adopted the tradition so that women had a coming-of-age ceremony as well as men. As an American, I should take advantage!

In less than an hour, I emailed my rabbi. "I'm in. Sign me up." I saw this as a chance to fill a spiritual void in my life. In the more practical sense, I wanted to address the lack I felt from not undergoing this significant rite of passage: that of officially becoming a Jewish woman, with all the attendant rights and responsibilities. In any case, I looked at this opportunity as a positive goal for me to work toward. The effects began immediately. Just being in the building brought me a sense of calm and peace and assurance that everything was going to be okay.

I had always prayed...like many people, especially when I wanted something. I had prayed, hard, when I was undergoing fertility treatments, asking to be given a child; most fervently, when I thought I might have a fatal disease; and again, during those long, lonely months, for the courage and strength to end my marriage. But I would not have called myself a religious person. I needed all the strength I could muster for what lay ahead: my own home, single motherhood. Surely God would help.

I showed up for the first meeting in a classroom with ten other adults on a Sunday morning at nine thirty a.m. They all had their own reasons for wanting to undertake this study. One woman had planned her bat mitzvah when she was a young teenager but had been stricken with mental illness and hospitalized; she'd had to drop out. As a now-stable adult, she was ready to recommit to the process. A lovely young woman was there because she was getting married to a Jewish man, recently converted, and was now looking to also take this next profound step forward. A sweet, serene older woman in her seventies had always wanted to be bat mitzvahed; it was not nearly as common for women in earlier generations. At this late stage in her life, she had decided to fulfill her lifelong dream.

A scholarly looking man had moved to the United States from Russia when he was in high school. He had not had a bar mitzvah ceremony, as his family had not been permitted to practice Judaism in his homeland. Another woman, very pragmatically, wanted to truly understand the prayers and not just recite them; she was seeking a firmer grounding in her faith. I was the only one undergoing a "change of life."

Our class ended at eleven a.m., which gave me fifteen minutes of free time before my daughter got out of her own Sunday school class. I fell into the habit of going into the sanctuary for those fifteen minutes to sit and pray for guidance and help. It was an amazing feeling: connecting to something bigger than myself. Safe. Serene. It was a feeling I had rarely felt in my life. There was something about it that reminded me of being a small child and spending time with my father...that secure, protected sort of feeling.

I felt such a sense of calm being in the presence of the rabbi and learning about the history of my people and our faith. The lessons reached and nourished something very deep inside me. I liked the other men and women in my class, and I enjoyed talking with them, but this was an experience that was truly all about feeding my own soul. It was such a different feeling to be sitting quietly in the temple, instead of rushing in like we did two or three times a year during the Jewish holidays, worried about parking, what we were wearing, being on time. This was quiet, reflective, an oasis in my chaotic life.

I followed through with my lessons. As the months passed they became more involved, with many more demands, including memorization, home study, and so on, but by then I was fully committed. It became somewhat of a running joke among my friends: "Congratulations on your womanhood!"

The day of my bat mitzvah was simply amazing. The ceremony—a b'nai mitzvah, for all ten of us—was beautiful. A program had been made up with each of our photos and a short explanation of why we had wanted to take this journey. I felt so close to all my classmates. I knew them intimately, and I cared about them. They inspired me. Temple Beth Sholom in Cherry Hill was full that Shabbat morning, packed to the rafters with friends and family all wearing their best. We all read different parts of the Torah. I sang a prayer with the cantor for the sick as my parents cried. It was surreal.

I wept throughout the day. I threw myself a disco party that night to celebrate my new life as well as my new status. I was surrounded by love and support. All my friends from every area of my life—work, other moms, my office team, my family, childhood friends—everyone I cared for was present. Well, Shane wasn't there.

But I was truly starting to come into my own...a much stronger and more grounded woman, ready to face whatever might come next. What had started out as trying to set a good example for my children had become a transformative journey for me.

CHAPTER 20

didn't particularly want to date, yet I kept pushing myself. Whenever my insanely overstuffed schedule would allow. I still missed Shane—his friendship, his insight, his warmth, his heart—but we hadn't spoken in months. At least for the foreseeable future, I needed to cut off all contact. Being friends with someone you still care for in a romantic way is torture. So: done were work assignments, friendship, everything. Over, finito, out. We had one final meeting at a Starbucks to settle a couple of outstanding articles coming up. After they were completed, he would work with someone else from my team. He broke down in the middle of the busy cafe, tears streaming down his face. I had to get up and get napkins. It seemed bizarre. I hadn't broken up with him—we never were "together" at all. We had just decided this wasn't our time and the platonic friendship we were trying to maintain was just too hard.

"Get out of your situation, I will be there for you. What else can I say?" I knew I needed to get on with my life. His girlfriend was so bad for him, but he wasn't budging. He said so. "I'm crazy to stay." He was. So we had to part ways, at least for the time being.

"Mommy is feeling down," I told my kids, when they asked why I seemed unhappy later that evening.

"Don't be sad, Mommy," Julian said. "You're so beautiful. You're going to marry me when I grow up!"

"You are going to marry a wonderful woman who loves you... but promise me you will always dance with Mommy," I told him, and gave him a huge hug.

Then along came a Jewish doctor named Daniel. A good guy friend of mine encouraged me to meet him. He was my age, also divorced, with kids close in age to my own. On paper he seemed like a "catch." But in reality, he was not—let's say—"ideal." After a handful of encounters, most of which included groups of friends, he had it in his head that I was going to be his girl-friend. He texted constantly. Patrolled my social media pages. Accused me of dating others—which to me made no sense, considering he was nowhere near the "boyfriend" lane.

Then one day, out of the blue, he took it upon himself to purchase an elaborate birthday gift for me. Only problem was, my birthday was more than two months away! Oh, and the gift was a diamond tennis bracelet. Extremely generous but also extremely inappropriate! I tried feverishly to have him take it back via the mutual friend who introduced us. Then it was suggested by my friend that I meet Daniel in person to discuss the gift and see if I still wanted to return it. I considered it for a second. But then..."No!"

Dr. Daniel was such a stalker. It was a very unhealthy obses-sion. Believe me, as someone who was enmeshed in my own unhealthy obsession, I still kept to certain standards. There were things I would not do, lines I would not cross. Daniel had no such compunctions. He persisted for a long time and I was relieved and a bit shaken when he finally let it go.

I still have the bracelet; Daniel absolutely refused to take it back.

* * * *

Marc texted again. "Are you in NY tonight?" This time, after months and months of random communications, I answered, "I will be later, why?"

"Want to get a bottle of wine and watch TV?"

"Absolutely not." I couldn't imagine anything worse than sitting around a twentysomething's bachelor apartment. Please! "But I will meet you at a bar for a drink if you like."

Okay! Nearly two years after I had met him on the train, we finally made plans to get together. "Listen, stop texting unless you need to cancel," I had to tell him. I had work to do! We met at a glorified college bar, a real dive, where I was carded at the door, which was hilarious. They carded everyone, because everyone in the crowd except me was in their twenties. Post-college/interning/first job stage. As I sat there all I could think about was my date from the week before.

I'd been set up by a work colleague. For a change, with an Upper East Side guy. Very successful, well-connected. He looked great for his age, which my friend estimated to be about fifty. Turned out he was fifty-seven, with kids in their early twenties. This wasn't going to work for me; the age difference was just too much.

"So, are we going back to your apartment?" he asked after two drinks and some light bites as we exited onto the street.

"Not exactly," I said.

He kissed me outside the restaurant; I got an uncomfortable flash of kissing my dad. "Bye!" I said brightly, and I took off running down the street, while he literally chased after me, calling, "I want another kiss, come back!" I could not believe it. This is the state of dating in New York!

That man could have been Marc's father. Back in the bar with the youngsters, Marc filled me in on what he'd been doing. He was now a hedge fund trader for a new company, a very established one and doing quite well. He was still cute. But not for me, and I told him so, to his face, over cheap beers. "Why can't we just hang out?" he asked.

"Because I am way past all that. You are going to date, get married, have kids.... I am not on the same path."

"I'm not even thinking about any of that right now."

"But I am!" I'm just a bit past the point of hanging out for the hell of it. I decided to set him up with my assistant. She still has plenty of time to kill. Single fortysomething moms with two kids don't! It's not as though I was rushing to remarry, but I certainly didn't want to just "hook up"—my time was too scarce and I'd rather have been spending quality time alone or out with my girlfriends if not with a man who had the potential for something more later on.

Even after this, he continued to reach out. A few days later he texted, inviting me to a horse race. I decided to go with a girlfriend and meet him there. And, in tandem, meet up with another guy—a very handsome and successful Upper West Side attorney I dated on and off. Why not? It's a good way to meet others. You never know!

So, there was Ryan—a New York trial lawyer, handsome, successful, never married, and no kids. He's quite serious, and I am not the most serious type, but everything else about him is awesome. I met him one night when I was out with a bunch of friends; we clicked. So far, so good.

The other guy's name was Steve. I met him through my friend Michele. They were platonic friends. He liked some of the photos he saw of us together, and she set us up. He was another lawyer, a real estate attorney/broker in New York City. He was so fun, so cute, the perfect age for me. Just a couple of dates so far, but it's been enjoyable.

And then there was Alex. Also, in real estate, also from New York City, very handsome, my age, never married, and very charming. None of these guys have ever married; not that uncommon for New York.

Despite the dating prospects and side-fun, I am still thriving alone. One of the most profound lessons I learned from this intermission was my innate ability to bring cheer and positive energy to those I love, those I'm surrounded by—even to myself. Through trial and error, setbacks and successes, I've worked hard, remained focused, and always tried to keep a smile on my face and a glow in my heart. I have a keen sense of sensitivity and the deep desire to heal those I care about and give love and light to all who need it most. My most sacred lesson during this time was gaining the ability to self-love. More than friends, more than family—I fell in love with myself. And I will never be the same.

Power Passage # 8

RUN FOR YOUR LIFE

"There will be days you don't think you can run a marathon. There will be a lifetime of knowing you have."
—RUNNER'S HIGH DAY-TO-DAY CALENDAR

I am not an athlete. Yes, I danced my whole life, and I stayed active with cheerleading and instructing aerobics, but I was by no stretch of the imagination a jock. I did not enjoy running, which was a big part of most sports. In my freshman year at Shawnee High School, my best friend, Heather, and I got the idea in our heads that we would join the spring track team, because we were looking to get in shape for swimsuit season. I was miserable going around and around that track. I quit two weeks in. Heather was made of tougher material; she made it through the end of the season.

I am not a quitter by nature. I hated giving up. But running was a bigger challenge than I could handle, and I was forced to admit it. The coach was more than happy to release me from the team. Actually, I'm sure he would have cut me had he been allowed to. That was it for running and me. Until...

Jason and I were separated but still living in the same house, which was hard on everyone's nerves. It felt like we were on top of each other all the time. One day, on the spur of the moment, I decided to go for a quick run. This was mainly about wanting to get out of the house. It was springtime, after a brutal winter; the most stressful winter of my life. Everything was closing in on me, and I needed a break. Just for a bit, and I didn't really have the time to get in the car and go somewhere. But, certainly a quick run was "acceptable," in my head, so out the door I went.

I just ran around my neighborhood for half an hour...and by ran, I mean I jogged for ten minutes, then walked for ten minutes. I had my music with me, earphones in, and it wasn't so bad. As I walked back into my house thirty minutes later, I felt better. For those thirty minutes my brain had quieted down. My worries and anxiety receded. I felt just a bit calmer and happier—healthier too. That was amazing. I started running several times a week.

One Saturday morning I was enjoying the music blasting in my ears...really getting into it, completely losing myself in the sound and the feeling of freedom. Five or six songs flew by and I didn't even realize it. I looked at my watch and realized thirty minutes had passed without my walking once. That small accomplishment really motivated me; it fired my competitive nature. I decided to increase my running time every day from that point on. Unbelievably, I started to really get into running.

I frequently saw friends posting on social media about their various runs. I did not do my usual due diligence and homework when it came time for my own race. Obviously, it would have been wise to attempt a 5K before jumping into a half marathon (13.1 miles of running pleasure) but I didn't put a lot of thought into it. When my friend Caryn posted that she had just signed up for the Disney half marathon in Florida eight months later, I thought it sounded fun. I've always loved Disneyworld, after all!

I reached out to my dear friend Jenice Armstrong at *The Philadelphia Inquirer*. She and her husband had been good friends of Jason's and mine. Now she spent a lot of time listening to me navigate my new life, not always so happily. "Would training with me and doing this run be something you're interested in?" I asked her. Jenice was a much more accomplished runner, having run in Philadelphia's Broad Street Run and other races for years. She was game, so we both registered for the half marathon.

We met frequently at area parks and running paths to train. We also ran independently but checked in with each other about our progress throughout the week. When I got serious about training for the race, I posted lots of inspirational photos on my social media. A pair of my beat-up running shoes, me running down the shore, stuff like that. My old friend Heather reached out…"You're running?" With the bulging-eyes surprise emoji. "No way!" I was the most unlikely runner, and she knew that firsthand. Most of my friends couldn't believe what they were seeing.

All of a sudden race day was upon us. I was heading back to Disneyworld, scene of many, many happy family memories. My friend, her husband, and I left for the race. It was time!

We registered and returned to the hotel for a good dinner; then we were up at four a.m. the next morning to get going. It was unseasonably cold that weekend, nearly freezing. As we milled around waiting for the race to begin, dressed in very thin clothing, I could not remember the last time I had been that cold. Jenice and I were not in the serious groups of hard-core runners; those groups were all ahead of the pack. We were way back in the corral, based on our expected times. Finally, we took off. There must have been twenty thousand people in that race. It was a mob scene.

Disney, of course, does not do anything halfway, and this half marathon was no exception. The Disney Run has become one of the largest and most popular running events in the country. It's a journey through the actual park, starting at Epcot, through the Magic Kingdom, with all the iconic characters on the sidelines to cheer the runners on and pose for photos. Many of the participants dressed up in actual princess costumes for the run; we were surrounded by tutus and tiaras, including our own.

Jenice and I practiced the Galloway Method, using her beeper that alerted us when it was time to switch from running to walking and vice versa. Jenice was a much stronger runner than I. She certainly could have run ahead of me. But that wasn't what it was all about. This was a very friendship-centric event for us; there were thousands of people there with their good friends, running together and celebrating as they made their way. Jenice and I finished the race with a respectable time of three hours, holding hands, crossing the line to a huge, cheering crowd. It was an absolutely euphoric feeling. We collected our precious medals and posed for photos in our sashes.

Every injury I'd ever had from my many years of ballet came back with a vengeance; my knee and ankle were killing me. Oh, my joints! Still, that did nothing to take away my joy. I was so incredibly proud of myself. Later that afternoon, Shane reached out to check on me. I was touched he remembered and he said he was proud, but I was even prouder. I was high on Princess Power. I ordered room service—fried chicken fingers and delicious steak fries with melted cheddar cheese—and absolutely inhaled it. I ate every delicious bite. I then treated myself to a massage and the three of us went out to dinner. We toasted to friends and our amazing accomplishment with a big glass of wine.

CHAPTER 21

║ truly believe that there has been a hidden, unseen hand at
║ work in terms of my career; that is, that everything in my
business life unfolded as it was meant to, according to some
grand master plan. I can't say I feel that way about my love
life—not at all—but I have faith that one day I will look back on
my relationships and say, "I understand." I already understand
why I am in public relations. My heart will always be in the news
business, but owning my public relations firm has blessed me
with opportunities I could not have enjoyed any other way. The
rewards it has brought me are endless.

When I was in the news world, I covered many disasters,
natural and man-made. For example, a local house burned down
due to faulty wiring and the owners lost everything. Every last
possession, down to their photos and papers burned to a crisp;
they barely escaped with their kids and lives. I never became
cynical enough for tragedies like this not to affect me. After the
camera turned off, I always tried to help steer the subjects—the
people of these stories—in the right direction: to assistance,
restitution, resources they may not have been aware of.

The nature of the business had us always rushing off to the next big story, the next disaster, the next fire or flood or whatever might come. I could do only so much. In public relations, I can really get much more involved in the subjects' lives. I have so many more resources at my fingertips. I know so many more people, and I know how to get the word out. This is truly my calling.

I always had a strong interest in medicine; I was a health reporter for much of my news career in addition to anchoring. When I started in public relations, I fell easily into "lifestyle" sorts of clients: boutiques, salons and spas, jewelers, beauty products, and so on. Several years down the road I signed my first doctor as a client, a plastic surgeon. As my business grew I became more confident in my abilities and became a much stronger salesperson for myself and my influence to help medical professionals expand their profiles and practices. It's a whole new world out there now, and doctors need PR just like everyone else.

Doctors and medicine eventually became somewhat of my specialty, which is the perfect fit for me. I love all my clients, but what's great about doctors is getting to pitch helpful and harder-news stories that will actually inform viewers and potentially help them. Fortunately, I'm not squeamish; I actually enjoy watching the procedures. I love seeing the befores and afters; I am perfectly happy in a hospital setting and having a bird's-eye view in the OR. I like all the medical shows I work with, from *The Doctors* to *Dr. Phil* to *Dr. Oz*. I feel that I still have a foot in news, even though it's PR. Of course, my doctors are also doing great things. In fact, they are changing lives.

I read about Shayna Richardson West in a tabloid magazine one day. While she was only in her early twenties, this young woman went skydiving. Her parachute did not deploy, and

Shayna landed flat on her face, breaking hundreds of bones and suffering serious internal damage. In the hospital where they were trying to save her, nurses discovered that she was pregnant, something she had not even known herself. Her unborn child also survived the accident.

Numerous plastic surgeries were required to repair the bones and reconstruct Shayna's face nearly from scratch. It had been terribly damaged. She was grateful for all the work so many fine surgeons put in to fixing her up. Her story got a great deal of national exposure; something about this really caught everyone's attention. "Pregnant Parachuter Survives Accident" blared the headlines. In a follow-up story I saw, she mentioned that one of the hardest things she had faced was the loss of her smile. She had broken most of her teeth upon impact; she now wore false teeth that she put in and took out every morning and night. For a young woman who had been noted for her beautiful smile, this was devastating.

I spoke with one of "my" doctors who was a periodontist. Dr. Alan Meltzer from Voorhees, New Jersey, offered to donate his time and materials to give Shayna a new smile...a permanent one, with implants. She accepted, and got a brand-new smile. She looked beautiful, she and her baby were both fine, and the doctor got some great PR. One year later, Oprah did a story on it. It was a heartwarming story. It was a win/win!

More recently, Dr. Steven Davis, a plastic surgeon I represent, was given a platform to show some work that really makes a difference. Gynecomastia is basically the medical term for "male breasts," a condition that often makes breast reduction surgery necessary—and it's a life changer. A young man named Hassan offered to serve as the face of this problem. While helping himself, he would hopefully inspire other young men in his situation to get help for what has been an embarrassing medical problem for many.

Hassan works as a truck driver; he's just a regular, really nice guy. He showed up at my office accompanied by his fiancée and their three-year-old son, and we shot a moving video about his "man boobs," as he called them. He was nearly shaking with nerves as he talked to our video camera and bared his chest. Hassan keeps his shirt on at all times, refusing to take it off for anyone. Even his fiancée had never seen him without a shirt on. "I have never shown anybody this before," he said.

He cried as he held his arms up and his fiancée lifted his T-shirt over his head to expose his upper body. His voice cracked as he recalled taping down his "boobs" with duct tape in high school, and how he was remorselessly bullied. This is actually not an uncommon condition, but it brings males so much shame. Body shaming is not just for women, as he and Dr. Davis discussed on their appearance on *The Doctors* I secured. Another win/win. After surgery, Hassan looked great!

The best thing about being in the news was trying to help people who had experienced one of the worst events of their lives. Similarly, the "helping" part of my job in PR is so rewarding. On top of that, the thing I love best about my business is that many clients have become dear friends of mine. Several even attended my bat mitzvah. These started as work relationships but have evolved into far more. I have a number of clients who are doctors, and with several of them we are now entering our second decade of business and friendship. I could not ask for more: being let into their business world but also into their hearts.

* * * *

I always want to have fun in the office. So, we do fun things, like have pajama day. I take the team on a corporate retreat a few times a year. I try to bring all the staff back treats whenever I go out of town. I often send the younger women in the office to the more fun, glamorous events in New York. PR and marketing are very woman-heavy industries. It was extremely gratifying to win an award from the National Association of Women Business Owners for being an outstanding woman in business. I was also awarded *South Jersey Magazine*'s "Reader's Choice" for best PR/marketing firm. I recently won an award by *CEO Report* for "Best Corporate Culture" for creating a friendly environment.

By this point I've learned by trial and error how to assemble a team and am blessed to have a good one around me. At one point I had two young associates who hated each other and were in my office every day, separately, both of them, to complain about the other. I did my best to straighten it out... but eventually I lost patience. There was a lot of mediating with millennials going on when I just wanted to get the job done. "You don't have to be besties, just do your job!" It's not always easy being the boss!

CHAPTER 22

I wake up on a Saturday morning, early. For a moment I'm disori-
ented. It's quiet without the kids, though I'm finally used to
our new schedule, where they are with me every other weekend,
in addition to three weekdays. Faintly, I hear the sounds of the
city: traffic, horns, garbage can lids clanging. I stretch, get out
of bed, and get moving. Light pours into the living room from
my floor-to-ceiling windows facing the Hudson River. I drink
in the view of the Manhattan cityscape. Soon enough my dog,
Max, and I are dressed in fashionista-worthy outfits and on
the street. We move easily along 42nd Street. I wave to the
guy at the newsstand, chat for a moment with the barista at
our favorite coffee shop. Then we move along and blend into
the crowd, just a girl and her dog, regulars in the city. Just like
every movie and TV show you've ever seen.

Moving to New York is something that would never in a
million years have happened had I not gotten divorced. An hour
and half away—two if traffic is really bad—and I am in another
world. One of the greatest destinations on the planet. My very
own slice of heaven!

Of course, I was long familiar with the city and its charms. I was a South Jersey girl; I attended Hofstra University on Long Island. Manhattan was always the big destination: for shopping, for culture, for nightlife...for absolutely everything. Many of my friends from college took off like a shot for the city the second they graduated. Because I wanted to be a television news anchor, I was destined to put in my time in various small markets in Podunk, USA, as far away as one could get from New York.

When I had a bit more control over where to put down roots, my husband was already well-established in business in Philadelphia, so that was obviously where we started. And thrived. Once I had two kids, the idea of city life receded into nothingness. We had carpools and soccer teams to worry about as we embraced suburban life.

* * * *

Now, I say that I "live in New York part time." Really what I did was rent an apartment. Still, in terms of life decisions, this ranked as one of the biggest I have ever made. In recent years I had started to go into New York City for work opportunities and new clients, and of course I loved every minute I spent there. The hustle, the energy, the feeling of being where it was at. The restaurants, the shopping, the landmarks. I fell so hard for urban life. I started to daydream about getting my own place there. I started to dream about happily ever after—for me.

The time spent in New York so far has been more than fun; it has begun paying off in a big way, business-wise. I signed some additional New York clients, in no small part because having my own established address went a long way toward establishing my credibility in that marketplace. It was time to really network, go after those big accounts, to take Manhattan, as they say.

I was also anxious to spread my wings a bit. Our new home—in the small town of Voorhees, where I had settled with the kids—was lovely, but like all small towns, it can sometimes be a gossipy community. I already felt that I knew everyone and they knew me. All about my kids, my divorce, my life. I had also established somewhat of a presence in the Greater Philadelphia area by that time, by virtue of my clients there and media I work with regularly. There was a real appeal in the absolute freedom and anonymity of New York City.

I had moved into my new home less than a year earlier; I was still putting the finishing touches on it. My parents were skeptical when they heard my big idea, worried about the expense. Worried I was taking too much on. Spreading myself too thin, financially, time-wise, everything. I was, but that has never stopped me before. The truth is that I got my new city place because I wanted to be there, so I made it happen. People seem to think that's an amazing accomplishment, but it really wasn't. I researched the options, I went apartment shopping, I got the lease reviewed by an attorney.... Step by methodical step, I crossed every *T* and dotted every *I*. I wanted my shot in New York. And what I want, I can get!

My original thought was to buy my own place there. Just a couple of preliminary trips with a real estate agent put a quick end to that idea, once I saw what I could afford. I could just about manage to swing a dorm room. A fairly nice dorm room, as they go, but a dorm room nonetheless. Not to mention that I was very aware of being on my own. I did not want to be responsible for any renovations; nor did I want to stress every time there was a leak or the AC went out in August. As a renter, all I had to do was make a call to the maintenance man. Blissfully, unlike at my house, none of those issues would be my problem. I would certainly pay dearly for this convenience, but I gambled that it would be worth it, and it was.

To finance this little real estate venture, I planned to rent out my property at the Jersey Shore I had retained in the divorce settlement (I had bought Jason out during negotiations). The condo was in Margate, a block and a half from the beach, an absolutely perfect location. I decided I would take that money and go to New York, even though I loved the shore. It was a tough decision.

One night over dinner a good friend and I were catching up, and I was telling her about my dilemma of holding on to it. It so happened she was looking for an investment, and we wound up partnering together to turn my property into a new venture for both of us. It's a beach-rental business that has gone very well. She's a great friend as well as an amazing business partner. Best of all, I kept my beloved place at the beach!

* * * *

Hell's Kitchen has recently become a trendy Manhattan residential neighborhood; what I loved about it from the start was that it is so walkable. The apartment I settled on is located near Midtown, toward the West Side. Location, to a New Yorker, is everything, and this was close to everything I wanted to do. It's within blocks of Times Square, so I can walk to all the Broadway shows. I can catch a matinee on Sunday afternoon on a whim. It's also close to Central Park and near the pier I love to run by.

The building itself is a forty-five-story high-rise with a doorman, with floor-to-ceiling windows in the unit's living room, offering spectacular city views. It came unfurnished, which to me was a plus. If there's one thing I love, it's decorating, and I can do it on the cheap too. Wayfair and Home Goods can transform any space! This particular empty space was such a blank canvas. I turned it into a very Kardashian-esque pied-à-terre, stark and dramatic, white and gray, gold and silver...with the view the main attraction. The monthly rent on this unfurnished one-bedroom was more than the mortgage on my house. I gritted my teeth and signed the first rent check, believing good things would come.

And come they did. It was so wonderful to be out on my own. Doing what I wanted, when I wanted, in my own little bachelorette pad. I started posting all over social media from my new place while I was out and about, and soon an old childhood friend reached out. Michele and I had been very close growing up but lost touch after middle school. She contacted me because she too lived in the city, and she and I reunited with ease and regained our bond of friendship immediately. It was great to have her back in my life! She also introduced me to my new and fast friend Andy. We have made many recent memories, even spending a New Year's holiday together in Mexico on a girls' trip.

Kristin, another old friend from high school, lives in New York too. None of these friends are married, and none have children. They all work in the fashion and beauty industries. They are quintessential "city girls." There's an entirely new and different kind of energy when I go out with these friends. It's a great complement to the strong friendships I maintain with the girls in my group of friends back home. I'm blessed to have so many amazing female friendships in my life! It's fun to be a singleton. Not that I'm looking to get crazy. Really, the wildest

I've gotten so far was going out to dinner with the girls, staying out until 11 p.m., and drinking a couple glasses of wine.

Arielle and Julian love the city. I like to bring them in for weekends, as a break from their suburban life. Absolutely, suburbia is great: Green grass. The trees. Clean air. My pool. Easy driving. Lots of rooms, instead of dividing our time between the front room and the back room of the apartment. Now we get to enjoy the best of both worlds.

As I walk down the streets in New York, or run in the park, I see older couples holding hands and talking animatedly. Or a cute young couple in athletic wear, coming home from their workout holding matching coffee cups. That's the happy ending we all want, including me! I haven't given up on it. I am all about being a good partner, and a best friend, and providing support. But that spark, that passion...I want it. I need it. If I don't have it, I'd prefer to be alone. I have plenty of support and love from my family and my girlfriends. I have two wonderful kids. I have some solid guy friends, and I have a growing business. If I am going to seriously date, I am going for that amazing, thrilling connection. It's invaluable to me, and worth fighting for.

But I am no longer willing to settle for less than I want and deserve. It's not about being married or having a boyfriend or anything else. I would much prefer to be on my own than unhappy. I can no longer settle for the potential someone shows or believe promises they make about the future. I need to see it—I need to deal with the man who is in front of me, doing whatever he's doing.

Today, more than two years after the divorce papers were signed and the dust has finally settled, I am thankful I made the leap. I am much happier and more fulfilled. Life is never perfect—there's always something—but I wish I had been braver earlier and just done it. It's truly not about finding someone else. I am much happier with Mindie. And that's the important thing, because that's whom I have to live with every day.

New York has given me everything; some dear friends are back. I established a stronger work presence there, which was important to be taken seriously in the city. In fact, business is going so well that I have started to look for additional official office space for my company. MB and Associates is on the rise!

Manhattan is my gift to myself. This life is something I would never be able to have if I was married. And I am not done dreaming.... Next on the list—LA!

ACKNOWLEDGMENTS

My editor, Julie McCarron, has been an enormous source of strength and insight during the entire writing process. She has guided me with her knowledge and perception about the publishing industry and given me the courage to share my story and reveal my true self. Julie has become both a professional sounding board and a personal one throughout the many twists and turns this book has taken. I'm proud that through Julie's reassurance, I was able to be brave enough to share intimate secrets to help others combat struggles and overcome the helpless feeling of being paralyzed.

Thank you to Anthony Ziccardi and the esteemed team of Post Hill Press for their faith in me and this project. Words could never express the sincere gratitude I have for Anthony as he wholeheartedly listened to my story and put his confidence in me, as well as providing me with tremendous and invaluable resources. I am so blessed to have become a member of this publishing team and will forever consider Anthony a dear friend.

Sincere thanks to my Post Hill Press editor, Rachel Shuster, for applying her incredible wit and writing finesse to my manuscript—taking it to an entirely new level of expertise. Much gratitude to Madeline Sturgeon for all her help and guidance with this project and the overall process.

Words cannot express my gratitude to Karen Ammond of KBC Media, who guided me down the literary path almost a year ago, putting me in touch with Julie to begin this journey. Karen has been a dear friend for decades and I will forever be indebted to her for the guidance she has given me.

Thank you to client and friend Paul Szyarto, who believed in my marketability and put me in touch with my publisher. Without that introduction I am not certain this book would have ever come to life—my appreciation goes beyond what words could ever express.

Thank you to my incredible team at MB and Associates Public Relations. Without their support this past year, I would not have been able to achieve this accomplishment. Their hard work, love, and support mean the world to me—as do they. They are not only devout employees but friends and family to me, and I'm most thankful for each and every one of them.

Thank you to my MB and Associates clients, past and present. They've trusted me with their good names and brands and enabled me to enjoy an incredible career and fulfilling professional life. I will be forever thankful to them and will always work harder than ever imagined to prove my value and worth.

Thank you to my incredible teachers. There are too many to name, but several from elementary school through college have inspired me and provided me with a deep sense of confidence which has given me the strength to climb mountains. Mrs. Kathy Moran and Ms. Stacy Kasse were both instrumental in nurturing my deep passion for the performing arts, which helped to steer me down my chosen career path. Mrs. Beverly Davis gave me the tools to write creatively, dig deep within myself to best express my thoughts, and fall in love with the English language. Writing is now my release and my passion, and I am so thankful to her for opening up my eyes to that world.

Thank you to my spiritual guides—Rabbi Micah Peltz, Cantor Jen Cohen, and Rabbi Steven Lindemann from Congregation Temple Beth Shalom in Cherry Hill, New Jersey. My sincere gratitude for encouraging me to embark upon my bat mitzvah studies and become a bat mitzvah after missing my traditional calling some thirty years ago. Being in their presence warms my soul and provides me with a comfort no words could ever express. They are all such an incredible force and I am so blessed to know them and have them as my spiritual leadership.

No acknowledgment would be complete without a sincere thanks to all my cherished friends. Some old and some new— they are all special and not a day goes by when I don't reflect and know how very blessed I am to have them in my life: Ali Smoller, Lauren Johnson, Jennifer Howard, Heather Summerville, Michele Pokrass, Kristin Franz, Stacy Scholnick, Joyce Evans, Jenice Armstrong, Tracy Sabol, Elizabeth Wellington, Sheinelle Jones, Jaimi Blackburn, Jessica Soffian, Heather Kramer, Cydney Long Penza, and so many more! I love them with all my heart.

Thank you to Jason for being my co-parenting partner, for being my friend, and for always being there for me whenever I need him. I thank him for allowing me to share my story—even the unpleasant parts—as he understands I truly want to inspire others to find their inner strength to make a much-needed life change. He will always be my family.

Thank you to my sister, Carolyn Kellerman, for her love and support through the years. Thanks for being my sounding board and always being there, no matter what the world has come to. We will always have each other to lean on, and I will forever be her rock and anchor.

My parents, Rick and Sandy Barnett, continue to guide me and provide me with a backbone whenever my own has wilted. I thank God every day for giving me such incredible role models to look up to. They have unselfishly provided me with a life and the resources I needed to excel, and I could never fully express how much I love them for that. Nothing they've ever done or continue to do for me goes unrecognized or unappreciated. I only hope to be half the parent to my own children that they are to me. I love them with all my heart and soul. They are without a doubt my biggest cheerleaders, and I will always strive to make them proud.

Lastly, my children, Arielle and Julian, while still very young, have taught me so much about life and love. They are both great mentors to me—even at an elementary school age—and I look to them in awe every day. They are both my light, my soul, and the reason I breathe. Everything I do is for the two of them as I want only to nurture them and provide them with the same fulfillment that they have given to me. They keep me grounded and smiling, and they teach me to appreciate all that life has to offer.